THIS TRAIN TERMINATES HERE

LONDON RAILWAY TERMINI UP TO 2020

JOHN JONES

DEDICATION

I dedicate this book to my darling wife Karen, my two fabulous children, Zak and Darren, my brother, Michael, and of course my parents, Brian and Christine Jones. All of whom have given me tremendous support and encouragement in everything I have ever achieved.

I would also like to mention Rosalind and Trevor Moore, as well as Matthew Jackson for their support whenever it was needed.

A special mention must also go to Tom Cressey, who has encouraged me and supported me throughout the writing of this book.

To you all, I say a massive thank you.

CONTENTS

ACKNOWLEDGMENTS

When you start writing a book, you have no idea how many people you need for it to be written. So, this list of people and organizations is not exhaustive, and if I have left anyone out, I am terribly sorry.

Firstly, a big thank you to Network Rail, c2c, Chiltern Railways, HS1 and Tfl. Without your permission to photograph and document your wonderful railway stations, this book obviously would not exist. Also, thank you to the many station staff which helped me along the way, your knowledge of the station you work at was invaluable in helping me find the more hidden gems.

Many thanks must also go to the authors of the books and websites which helped me research the mini history sections. They are fully referenced in the bibliography at the end of this book, which is also where you will find details of the sculptures, statues and items of interest contained within this book.

Finally, thank you to the people who inspired me to realize that I could get out there and compile a book of this nature. This particularly applies to Geoff Marshall and Vicki Pipe, whose 'All the Stations' series on YouTube proved that, if you are dedicated enough, anything is possible. Also to Michael Portillo, whose 'Great Railway Journeys' television programme produced for the BBC, has shown the variety in the United Kingdom's railway stations; something which I hope I have replicated for the London termini contained within this book.

INTRODUCTION

The London terminus. The start or end of a journey. How many of us use these giants of the UK Railway network? Perhaps as a commuter, rushing to get to work, meeting that important client, getting that hot beverage of choice on the way. Or as a day tripper, eager to see the sights of London, or even dinner and a show? And of course, then arriving back at the terminus, getting a quick bite to eat and something to drink before finding that platform which has the train which will take you home.

How many of us have done exactly that, taking the role of the London terminus station for granted? Its purpose, it seems, just to get us all from A to B in the most efficient way possible. But how many people bother to stand a while and look around at the magnificence of these buildings? How many of us take the time to appreciate the history around them? Have you just passed through a terminus, not seeing past the ticket barriers or information boards to find what else is around you?

To be honest, I have. It is just so easy to have your head down, just looking for that exit, be it to the outside, or to the Underground station below. In this day of the mobile device, many are seen moving through the concourse, head down reading the latest tweet or Facebook entry. I have been guilty of this.

But these places of hustle and bustle in some cases yield much history. Many are architectural masterpieces, while others are purely functional. Yet all are fascinating pieces of engineering and organization. Without them, modern London would possibly not be able to fully function.

Within this book my aim is to bring you, the reader, the wonder of the fourteen current designated London termini, with brief histories and walkthroughs of each one. Whether it be the cosmopolitan European feel of St Pancras International, or the pure commuter rush of Charing cross. Marvelling at Brunel's grandeur masterpiece Paddington, or the intimate feel of Fenchurch Street. I hope to get us all to stop at least occasionally and appreciate the marvel of the London terminus. A place which many of us just think of as 'the end of the line'.

This book provides walkthroughs that were current up to the middle of 2020. I hope that many of the stations have the same layout when you are reading this, but if not, I hope that they at least help you to find some of the hidden gems contained within these marvels of 19th Century architecture. Stations are ordered by passenger entry / exit figures for 2018 /2019, from smallest to largest.

In writing this book, I have tried to be as clear and concise as possible. However, I do realise that many readers may not know the many acronyms or words, some of which are unique to the British Railway network. For that reason, here is a small list of some of the more common terms used, which should help you better understand not only this book, but the wider railway in this country.

- **3rd RAIL -** Electrification of the railway by means of a 3rd rail, usually beside one of the running rails. Common in the UK in the South East of the country
- **AWS -** Automatic Warning System - An in cab warning system for use in Block Signalling operations. A disc inside the cab either shows black, which means the signal approaching is green, or is yellow/black (in the style of a sunflower) which indicates the next signal is at caution (yellow/double yellow) or stop (red). A horn will sound inside the cab to indicate the next signal is not green, and the diver will have to push an acknowledgement button within 2.75 seconds, otherwise emergency brakes will be applied. The indicator will then change from black to "sunflower", and remain like this until a green signal is approached, where it will change to black again.
- **CATENERY -** Overhead wires which power a train, via a **PANTOGRAPH** on the train.
- **DEMU -** Diesel Electric Multiple Unit - a train which can use both diesel and electric power. An example of which is the British Rail class 205 unit which worked in the South East of the UK between 1957 and 2004, and which were part of the British Rail "slam-door" stock.
- **DLR -** Docklands Light Railway - a railway system in London which uses driverless trains.
- **DMU -** Diesel Multiple Unit - a diesel only train, many in use at time of writing, such as the 153 unit seen on many rural lines in the UK.
- **DOWN -** Typically the railway line moving **away** from London.
- **DSD -** Drivers Safety Device - a switch on the floor which the driver must keep depressed in order to enable the train to move. Think of it as a dead man's switch, if it is not depressed, then the train cannot take power.
- **EMU -** Electric Multiple Unit - a train solely powered by electricity.
- **PANTOGRAPH -** Located on the roof of a train or locomotive, connects to a **CATENARY** to provide power.
- **RAKE -** more than one coach or wagon coupled together will form what is known as a Rake.
- **TOC –** Train Operating Company, such as SouthEastern or LNER
- **TPWS -** Train Protection and Warning System, advance system of the **AWS.**
- **UP -** typically the railway line moving **Towards** London.

Moorgate

Opened : *1865*
Platforms : *4 (2 currently operational)*
Underground Lines : *Circle, Hammersmith & City, Metropolitan, Northern (City Branch)*
Current TOC : *Great Northern*
Entry and exit figures 2018/2019 : *11,508,936*

The smallest of the London termini, Moorgate is often overlooked as a terminus, mainly due to its close proximity to Liverpool Street. Primarily an underground station, its two national rail lines utilise the East Coast mainline to Welwyn Garden City. Full of abandoned passageways and tunnels, mainly due to extensions which were started but never finished, it is nonetheless an important part of London's termini structure.

A brief history

The nearby then terminus of Farringdon would get a new station east from it in 1861 called 'Moorgate Street'. Run predominantly by the Metropolitan Railway, it would soon see traffic from other companies. In fact, an increase in goods traffic would see the line widened, and in 1866, four lines entered the station. This carried not only goods and passenger traffic from the Great Northern Railway to Kings Cross, but also services run by the Midland Railway to Kentish Town.

The City and South London Railway opened a line between Stockwell and Moorgate Street in 1900, after a protracted process lasting nearly seven years. This would be extended to Angel in 1901. More expansion in 1904 saw services to Finsbury Park, run by The Great Northern and City Railway, and this was called 'The Northern City Line'. It was connected to the rest of the station via escalators. The main difference in this line was the tunnels were larger to allow mainline trains, something which would prove to be greatly beneficial later on. It also was the first to have automatic signalling. Although popular at the start, declining numbers meant that by 1913, a planned extension to the Great Northern Railway mainline never came to fruition.

The station was renamed Moorgate in 1934, with connections to Euston and Camden town also in that year. In the 1960's the station was completely modernised and a total of 6 platforms (mixed of Underground and British Rail) were now in operation. When British Rail came to Moorgate, they used steam engines, but were slowly replaced by non-corridor electric locomotives until the mid-1970's when they were replaced by full corridor class 313 stock.

One of the darkest days in London Undergrounds history unfortunately happened at Moorgate on 28th February 1975, when 43 people died and 74 injured when a train on the southbound Northern City Line crashed into the dead end at the tunnel past the platform. It took just over 2 weeks to clear the wreckage and the station re-opened on 6th March. A commemorative plaque is at the station, and this is covered in the walkthrough section.

1982 saw overhead electrification, which allowed services to run from Bedford to Moorgate. This was overseen by Thameslink, and lasted until 2009 when the major Thameslink upgrade was started. Great Northern currently run trains to Hertford and Welwyn Garden City, and new trains came into service in 2019, replacing the 40 year old stock.

The Elizabeth Line platforms at Liverpool Street will be very close to Moorgate station, and it has been decided that an interchange will be built to the Northern line platforms at Moorgate, as well as the Central Line platforms at Liverpool Street. This should increase passenger traffic, and hopefully give more prominence to this small, yet important terminus.

The railway station in 2020

Let us start outside the station, which in itself has three entrances, one in Moorfields and two in Moorgate Road, either side of the roadway. Before entering, turn into Moor Place, and you will see a plaque on the wall. This commemorates the disaster which took place in 1975. Incidentally, if you turn back towards Moorgate Road, turn left and go up here for around 5 minutes you will see a park opposite you called Finsbury Square. It is here, in 2013, that a memorial stone was unveiled detailing all who died in the disaster, as well as dedications for the emergency services and survivors. If you have time it is well worth a visit to view and reflect.

Getting back to the plaque on the wall, turn to your right and head towards Moorgate Road, then turn left and enter the Underground station. Immediately you will see the entrance on the other side in Moorfields! This highlights how small the station is. A small retail shop is on your right and stairs are located on your left in the middle of this mini concourse.

Going down these, you will see a sign ahead of you which either directs you either to go right if you already have a ticket, or to go left if you require tickets. Let us assume you do not have a ticket, and turn left at the bottom of these stairs.

Ahead of you now, under a very low ceiling, you will see a small kiosk. Go towards this and then turn left. You will see exit gatelines ahead of you, and further on, ticketing machines on the wall as you go around again to the left. Another set of gatelines, this time for entry, is ahead of you.

Let us now assume you are wishing to gain access to the National rail platforms, so go through these gates. Ahead you will see escalators to the Northern line, with access to the Hammersmith and City and Circle lines just ahead and to your left. But we will turn immediately right here and follow the signs above to the National Rail platforms. As you go under the sign and turn right, a Lovely staircase awaits you. This is covered either side in blue rectangular glossy tiling and is quite stunning in comparison with the rest of the interior!

At the bottom of this small flight of stairs, you will start to descend a spiral staircase, until you reach a landing area which will take you onto the National Rail platforms. Carrying on down this staircase would take you to the northern line platforms. There is also an escalator between the National Rail platforms which will take you to the Northern Line.

Overall the look of these platforms is that of an Underground station, which is not surprising given the history. At the end of each platform are buffers plus an extended overrun into the blocked off tunnels.

In the rest of this book, I will dedicate a small section after each mainline station walkthrough to the Underground station. But I will make an exception in Moorgate's case as the main concourse is effectively the underground station as well. The main points are that the Northern Line can be accessed via the National Rail platforms via the escalators which are situated between the platforms, as previously stated. They can also be reached via an escalator which is opposite the gateline near the ticketing office.

Access to the Circle, Hammersmith and City and Metropolitan Line is made via a set of escalators which can be reached either by the gateline by the ticketing office (by making a slight left when going through). Alternatively if you came down the stairs from street level, as detailed in the station walkthrough, you could take a right at the bottom and go through the gatelines which are ahead of you. Obviously, you can only do this route if you have a paper ticket, or are paying by using an oyster or credit/debit card.

In conclusion

Moorgate, although the smallest termini, is worth a quick look, if only for the quirkiness of it all. The stunning blue staircase leading to the spiral staircase as you descend to the National Rail platforms, gives this station a bit of identity. Moorgate should also be busier once the connection to the Central and Elizabeth lines at Liverpool Street is complete.

Blackfriars

Opened : *1886 (as St Pauls)*
Platforms : *4*
Underground Lines : *Circle, District*
Current TOC's : Thameslink, SouthEastern
Entry and exit figures 2018/2019 : *12,139,538*

The only London terminus which can legitimately be described as being on the river Thames. The modern platforms here sit on Blackfriars bridge, flanked by two station buildings both north and south of the river. A station which is designed for the commuter, it now also caters throughout the day for passengers wishing to travel to London and through to Luton via the re-established Thameslink route.

A brief history

The history of Blackfriars is a fairly complicated one. The London, Chatham and Dover railway company opened a station called Blackfriars Bridge in 1864 on the south side of the Thames. It was designed from the outset at a through station which would eventually reach Farringdon on the north side of the river. However delays to the construction of both the road and rail bridge would mean the station would be a terminus for the first six months.

The bridge finally opened in 1865, and had large, decorated buttresses with the LCDR coat of arms at each end. These have been preserved and sit on the south side of the river, near the entrance to the south station building opposite the road bridge. Another station, Ludgate Hill was opened in the same year on the north side of the river, and further extensions to Farringdon and Kings Cross occurred sometime later. Ludgate Hill did not last long however, closing in 1929.

Confusingly, their rival company, the South Eastern Railway, also opened a station between London Bridge and Charing Cross. They called it 'Blackfriars Road'. This station only lasted 5 years, when it was replaced by the still operating Waterloo East Station.

Another 20 years would pass until the LCDR gained a new terminus, this time north of the river. It was called 'St Pauls', and inside the station an elaborate sandstone wall was erected detailing destinations which 'could' be reached. These included not only places like Margate and Dover, but more exotic ones like St Petersburg and Marseille! The wall has been preserved and can be seen in the north station building at Blackfriars today.

The sandstone wall was the only elaborate item however, as the cash strapped LCDR could only afford a modest building in red brick, with rather small towers, and it seemed squashed against the viaduct. It had three terminating tracks and two through tracks, the latter tracks running around an island platform.

With the new station came a new bridge, almost adjacent to the old one. Once this was opened, Blackfriars Bridge station was closed to passengers, although it still remained a goods depot up until 1964.

In 1899, the LCDR merged with the SER, and was then known as the South Eastern and Chatham Railway. This in turn became the Southern Railway in 1923, and in 1937 St Pauls Station was re-named to 'Blackfriars'. The original bridge was still standing up until 1985, when it was removed due to excessive deterioration in the wooden structure. The pillars still remain though, partly because it was too expensive to remove them, and removal may have caused damage to the new bridge.

Although a few improvements were seen in the 1970's, namely a new entrance hall and access to the underground station, it was the period between 2009 and 2012 which saw the biggest redesign of the station in 100 years. Part of what was known as the 'Thameslink' programme would see the station change into a modern design, with a unique platform configuration which spanned across the existing bridge, which itself was extended using the set of original pillars next to the bridge. These were clad in concrete.

The three terminating platforms were reduced to two and the through platforms now run through using their own platforms, albeit on the opposite side to where they once were, and were extended to accommodate the new 12 car Thameslink 700 class trains. The roof over the bridge is covered with solar panels which provide up to 50% of the power to the entire station. In addition a new entrance on the south side of the river was also constructed.

The capacity was increased from 12 trains an hour to up to 24, with Thameslink currently providing the majority of through traffic and SouthEastern mainly providing the terminating services.

The railway station in 2020

Blackfriars station has three distinct entrances, one to the north and two to the south of the river Thames. However there is another 'hidden' entrance on the north side, but we will get to that much later. Getting between them using the platforms is not an option (unless you have a travelcard type ticket). So because of this, we will start on the north side of the river at the impressive glass fronted entrance on the corner of Queen Victoria Street and Victoria Embankment. This building was part of the complete refurbishment which was completed in 2012.

Entering here you will see an obviously great internal space, flooded with natural light. To your left are tickets for the Underground, as well as an Oyster top up machine. To your right are stairs up to platforms 2, 3 and 4. If you carry on forwards into the space, the roof comes down to a white ceiling with quite unique round lights. Escalators and lifts to platforms 2, 3 and 4 are to your right, and ticketing machines are to your left. A small way further forward will bring you to ticketing windows on your right.

Keep moving forward and the toilets are forward and to the left at the end of this mini concourse. Of more interest however is the big sandstone block which dominates the wall at this end. It contains many of the places which you could get to by train and was part of the original station. It survived the bombing of the Second World War, and is an impressive and unique sight. Not only are many South East towns featured, but also European cities like Antwerp and Florence. Alongside this to the right are plaques for a Civic Trust award in 2014, for Dick Whitwell who was part of the Thameslink team who worked on the Thameslink project, and finally one explaining the sandstone blocks.

There are now some stairs and escalators which take you up to platform 1. You can go up here and look out over the river, but a gateline will stop you going all the way across it (unless you have a ticket). But it is a good place to just view the engineering achievement here. The roof structure is made up of many solar panels, and is one of only three such bridges in the world. The railway dips under the city after exiting the station at the northern end. Once you have had a look, head down the stairs and out through the glass entrance we came in earlier.

Turn to your left and start to go across the river on Blackfriars road bridge. You will notice red pillars in the water alongside the new bridge. These supported the old bridge; you can see that the third pillar was incorporated into the design of the new bridge. Carry on over the bridge and at the end you will see the very impressive coat of arms, fully restored and very colourful. It is for the London, Chatham and Dover railway, and there were two of them at either end of the bridge.

After going past these coats of arms, turn right down some steps so that you are now going alongside the river. After a while you will come to the first of two entrances to the station on this side of the river. Do not enter this one, but instead keep walking along the river path.

Eventually, this walkway opens up and you will see ahead of you the station entrance for the south side. This small, modern, almost circular structure was also constructed as part of the Thameslink programme. Immediately upon entering there is a coffee shop in front of you, and a few places to sit on the right. Moving further in there is a small departure board in front of you, and natural light floods in from the glass to your right and from skylights above.

Going through a square arch, you will enter a small concourse, with a ticketing area. Turn to your right and look up to see a nice mosaic style picture on the wall, which uses cut out figures against a railway ticket background, the figure on the extreme right seems to be a soldier. This space is quite airy with a large ceiling, but you can only get up the stairs with a ticket as there are barriers in the way. If you continue down here you will come to the entrance we saw earlier, and this will take you to the steps and up onto Blackfriars road bridge once again.

Now I did mention an additional entrance on the north side of the river. This entrance is in Puddle Dock Lane, and can be reached by doing the following. Come out of the north side entrance and turn right, going down Queen Victoria Street. You will pass under the railway and alongside a grey office block on your right. As you come to a small road in front of you, you should see some steps on your right. If you go up these stairs you will see to your right the bronze fronted entrance to Blackfriars station. This was put here in the 1970's, as British Rail had offices here, but you can still go through here and after a couple of turns you should find yourself with platform one ahead of you. Unsurprisingly this entrance is not very busy, and if you need platform one and are near this location, then it is a nice little shortcut.

The underground station

On entering the station building at the large glass frontage at Victoria Embankment (North side), the underground station gatelines will be in front of you. There really is nothing of note here as unless you have a ticket, that is pretty much it! For completeness though, I will say that once going through the gateline you should turn right for the Westbound platforms of the District and Circle lines, or left, which will take you to the Eastbound District and Circle lines. Having said that, if you were just an Underground passenger at Blackfriars, either entering or exiting from this cavernous glass entrance would be one of the more modern spectacles on the Underground network.

In conclusion

London Blackfriars is a unique station. Having the platforms run across the river makes clever use of space, and the solar panels make it at the time of writing the most self-sustaining mainline station in the UK. The fact you can enter and exit both sides of the river makes it a good choice for the commuter. It does still retain some of its charm, and if you look, even some of its heritage is on display. With the completion of London Bridge Station, it seems that both stations complement each other, and help the Thameslink vision come to fruition.

London Marylebone

Opened : *1899*
Platforms : *6*
Underground Line : *Bakerloo*
Current TOC : *Chiltern Railways*
Entry and exit figures 2018/2019 : *16,146,552*

The last terminus to be built in London, Marylebone is a project which allegedly has never been finished. Designed with future expansion in mind, the station is one of the quietest termini, its six platforms only becoming busy during the rush hours, or when there is a major event happening at the nearby Wembley Stadium.

But herein lies its charm, with an enchanting roof, train shed and concourse. It has very wide platforms, and nods to its past are extensive if you take the time to look. In fact one may say it is a place to sit, and reflect in its relative quiet.

A brief history

The station was built for the Grand Central Railway, which was previously the Manchester Sheffield and Lincolnshire Railway. The terminus for this was at Canfield Place, just north of London Zoo, but the company wanted to extend further into the heart of London. Although this was to be only two miles away, it came with a host of planning problems.

Sir Edward Watkins pushed the vision of the new terminus forward when he became director of the railway in 1864. A true visionary, he believed in connecting the railways, eventually feeding them into a channel tunnel connecting England with France. This forward thinking idea however was rejected by parliament in 1882, as parliament was fearful that it would leave Britain vulnerable to invasion. He also wanted his railway to be a fast, new ninety-two mile route from Nottingham to London, via Buckinghamshire and Harrow.

However, his idea to quickly build the new terminal for his railway was held up many times by planning objections. The most notable was that from the MCC at Lords Cricket Ground. The original plans had the railway going straight though the Nursery end of the ground. The owners of the ground, the MCC, were adamant that they were not going to give up their £100,000 investment. After many years of argument, it was eventually agreed that the railway company would purchase and relocate the orphanage next door to the ground. This would enable them to use a 'cut and cover' technique to build two tunnels under the far end of the Cricket pitch. The pitch was reinstated as before, and the MCC would also build on the site of the former orphanage.

All this work was started in August 1896 and completed in 1898. It was during this work that the railway adopted its new 'Grand Central Railway' title. The new company, proud of this new name, would have it adorned almost everywhere at the new Marylebone terminus. It was on the walls, on the archways and on the many Iron gates at the property.

The terminus itself was not the grandest, the majority of the money being spent on the railway infrastructure. Designed by the railways chief engineer, Henry Braddock, a four platform trainshed was erected, covering only 495ft of the 950ft platforms. A roof also covered the main concourse, although this was obscured by a white plastered ceiling in the main ticketing hall. Above this ticketing hall were offices for the committees and board, who moved here in 1905 from Manchester.

The concourse was vast considering the small number of platforms available. It was originally planned that six or more platforms were to be in the terminus from the outset, but money constraints prevented this. It was not until the 21st Century that more platforms would be added.

Connection to the London Underground system was via the Bakerloo line when it extended from Baker Street in 1907. Originally named Great Central, it was changed to Marylebone in 1917 after much discussion with the railway company.

Like most London termini, a grand hotel was also built. It sits across the road from the station in Melcombe place, with a main entrance on Marylebone Road. Access to the station is by small entrance in Melcombe Place via a very ornate covered walkway to the main ticket hall. This hotel rivals that of the one at St Pancras in its opulence. It has a vast central atrium inside, and some say it is the finest of all the London railway hotels. Having been a hotel for more than 40 years, it would however become the offices for the Midland Region of British Rail from 1945 until 1986. It was converted back to a hotel in 1993 and is currently owned by the Landmark Hotel Company as the Landmark London Hotel.

From the outset, the station was not busy. The relatively nearby stations of Euston and Kings Cross / St Pancras took passengers up to the north of the country, and had done for around 50 years at most. However its adjoining freight depot proved to be very busy, which meant that most trains were goods. In fact it had the largest freight depot in London, being twenty eight acres in size.

During the late 1950's and through the 1960's Marylebone was looked at for closure on many occasions. The express services finished in 1960 and freight operations suffered the same fate five years later. The main line north was cut under the 1966 Beeching review, and now the station only served trains as far north as Birmingham, and west to Aylesbury. Calls in 1971 to close it were shelved, but low passenger numbers in 1982/83 lead to new calls for the station to be shut (there was even a plan to turn the trackbed into an expressway for coach traffic).

It did however survive, when in 1986 British Rail established a new working group for the line. This enabled the station to be more adventurous with its timetabling, with more heritage, excursion and special event trains being run. In 1996, Chiltern Railways took over when franchises started, and they have been running the railway here ever since, even utilising the class 68 locomotive to haul trains.

The future is bright for this sleepy station, and the work done by Chiltern Railways to preserve the infrastructure here is amazing. Indeed the whole roof was refurbished in 2011 with new glass and sheeting, preserving the Grade II listed structure for many years to come.

The railway station in 2020

Entering via the main entrance at Melcombe Place, you will see on your right a pole with the British Rail symbol, Chiltern Railways logo and the Underground roundel on a single long cube in a bronze colour. Directly in front is the impressive station entrance, two smaller arches alongside a main archway. To note here is the writing of Marylebone Station above the arch, and you will still see an uncoloured Network SouthEast logo next to the word station.

A taxi rank and drop off area is also here, underneath a very ornate canopy which has black pillars broken up with a red leaf motif around a third up from the ground. This is certainly the grandest taxi rank of all the London termini. The impressive London Landmark hotel is opposite the station here, with an entrance under the canopy.

Moving towards the main entrance, note the blue gates with 'GCR' in gold, denoting the Great Central Railway. This can also be seen on a small crest above the main archway, below the words 'Marylebone Station' This yellow brickwork is in excellent condition, and sets the scene for what you are about to see inside.

As you look forward, the station opens out and you can see the platforms directly ahead, under the spectacular roof which spans the concourse. To your right here are a couple of retail and food outlets. To the left of you is the electronic information board showing departures and arrivals, as well as a digital clock. Underneath this are electronic ticket machines, and you will see a small food outlet just further on. Just behind you are the Female and first set of accessible toilets, to the left of flower retailer (at time of writing). These are still currently charged for, unlike the Network Rail managed stations.

Let us turn left here and go past the departure/arrival board (which will now be on your right). As you look forward you will see the station office in the middle of the concourse; this also serves as the information centre. Move up to this information centre slightly and you will see more electronic ticket machines slightly ahead and to the right of you. Of note here is the continuation of the old network SouthEast branding, this time in the familiar red blue and silver colouring.

Move towards these machines, and then turn to your right. In front of you now will be the ticket office, set within an original looking yellow brickwork. It is nice to see that the station still has these little touches to its past. If you now look to your left, you will see the entrance to the Underground station, which is weirdly a much more modern affair!

Turn back to the central information centre, move towards it and then turn right to go down a part of the concourse which is lined with retail outlets. Cash machines can be found on the right hand side. On your left, a major retailer (currently M&S) is housed within the old ticket hall, and halfway down here (still on your left on one of their entrances), there are three plaques on the wall.

The top one is the coat of arms of the Great Central Railway. Below that is a blue Plaque dedicated to the centenary of the birth of Sir John Betjeman, dated 2nd September 2006. The Plaque below this one has a green outer ring with a red tablet inside. It is to mark the Centenary of Marylebone Station in 1999, and was unveiled by the son of Edgar Fay, the general manager of the Great Central Railway from 1902 to 1922.

Turn back away from these and head down the concourse, away from the information centre. A telephone kiosk is on your left as you go down here, along with advertising boards which wrap around the pillars. Near to the end you will see a bench, and this has a further three plaques on the wall above it. These contain dedications to those employees who lost their lives in the first world war.

From left to right, the plaques are as follows. The first set in a bronze sheet with wood surround is in memory of employees of the engineers office at Marylebone who lost their lives in the First World War. Below this is a larger plaque, also a bronze sheet on a wooden frame. This is dedicated to the employees of the Goods office who died in the First World War. The last one is white

marble set on grey marble. It is dedicated to members of the Great Central Railway London and District Goods staff who died in the First World War. Unsurprisingly, these plaques are in impeccable condition, and are a credit to the current owners who keep them that way considering they are not guarded in anyway whatsoever.

Carrying on past the plaques, the gents toilets are on your right. Currently as of 2020, and like the female ones, they are still at cost to the traveller (30p at time of writing). As previously said, this is at odds with the Network Rail managed stations in London who completely abolished the charges in 2019.

If you now go through under an archway, you will encounter a public house and then to the exit to Harewood avenue. Before you exit though, on your right are various pictures hanging on the wall. These detail the history of the railway station and have old style lighting illuminating them from above. A nice hidden gem, and if you have time to do so a really good read.

Outside this exit on the wall is a clear plaque with the Chiltern Railway logo on it, as well as the underground roundel and details on the station operating times. To your right above you is a white sign with the British Rail logo with Marylebone Station written below it. This sign also contains the Chiltern Railways logo and the Underground Roundel.

Move back into the station, and before you go through the arch onto the main concourse, a small departure board is hanging on your right hand side. Go through again onto the main concourse, but try to look up to appreciate the mainly glass roof. Moving towards the end again, go past the central information board and turn left. Here you will see the gatelines for all platforms. The view from here is superb, with the fabulous trainshed roof extending out in front of you. The bright red columns holding the roof are beautifully ornate, and the left hand columns have electric lights in pairs running down the trainshed.

If you are able to do so, go through the gatelines. The space is nice and wide on the left, and a little way down platform 3 there is an enormous bike rack which goes almost two thirds along the side of this platform. Also here (and on the main concourse too) is a nice touch by Chiltern, and that is coffee cup recycling stations. A great idea, and judging by how full they were, very well used by the passengers.

If you have the time, go out of the train shed along the platform and take a look back at the station. It may not be the largest of the London termini, but the stunningly refurbished quaint roof is very well proportioned, and is certainly a fantastic sight.

The underground station

Marylebone Underground Station is a very easy affair, as there is only one tube line here, the Bakerloo Line. The entrance is on the main station concourse as described above, left of the ticket office. Escalators will take you down to a corridor which you follow until you get to two sets of stairs which will take you down to the platforms. An overbridge connects these and has four semi-circular riveted designs along it. The colour scheme throughout is cream and green.

Of particular note is the 'Grand Central' tile mosaic on the northbound platform. This of course refers to the original owners of the station. Unfortunately at time of writing Marylebone has no step-free access. Other than that, it is one of the easier London termini underground stations to describe as it only has the one Underground line!

In conclusion

Marylebone is a medium sized but very architecturally pleasing station. From the quaint entrance with the covered taxi rank, to the trainshed with its very ornate pillars. The station reflects the towns it serves, refined but with a hint of laid back about it. The current TOC, Chiltern Railways, have done a good job in keeping the station looking fantastic, all the while looking after the heritage.

Also of note is that Chiltern Railways have not (at time of writing at least) ditched the Network South East branding, which can be found in the booking hall area. I for one hope it is kept, as a reminder of the past. After all many other artefacts from the Grand Central Railway are here, so why not.

The station is generally quiet during the daytime, and so, If you can, try to spend some time here. Perhaps find a table by a café, sit and enjoy the surroundings in one of the best medium sized termini anywhere in the country.

Fenchurch Street

Opened : *1841*
Platforms : *4*
Underground Lines : *None*
Current TOC's : *c2c*
Entry and exit figures 2018/2019 : *18,507,676*

Tucked away in the City of London is this small terminus, mainly serving the eastern county of Essex. The furthest point away from the end of the platforms is only 39 ½ miles. It also has the unenviable status as the only London terminus not to have a direct underground link.

However due to its position near the heart of the city, together with the close proximity of the new high rise properties such as the 'Gherkin' and 'walkie-talkie' (the latter having a spectacular sky garden), make it an important terminus for that part of the country. It is also very architecturally pleasing, and being tucked away in a small cul-de-sac, one of the quieter London termini in terms of noise.

A brief history

The London and Blackwall railway line was placed mainly upon a brick viaduct, to minimise demolition in this already built up area of London. Running only between what would be Fenchurch Street to Blackwall, due to the closeness of the stations, the line was operated using cable traction on a 5ft gauge railway. This service operated from 1840 from a temporary terminus called "The Minories". The practice continued until the actual terminus was completed in 1841 at a cost of £250,000. The name of this new terminus would be "Fenchurch Street".

A few years later, it had a grand new entrance built which was designed by George Berkeley, and opened in 1853. A semi-circular roadway was laid to link it with the main road, and this was named Fenchurch Place. The building frontage is still standing today, and it really is in juxtaposition amongst the high rises of the current city skyline. A lovely iron and glass trainshed mimicked the archway on the top of the station building, stretching 300ft along the concourse and platforms.

It was envisioned that eventually a line to the Eastern Counties railway would be laid, and this was indeed the case when a new service commenced with the London, Tilbury and Southend railway taking charge of operations. In 1856 a full service to Southend and Tilbury from Fenchurch Street started, and in 1881 an express service would take passengers from Southend to Fenchurch Street in one hour.

1923 saw the London and North Eastern Railway take control of the station, and the growth of traffic along the Southend Line ensured a £250,000 investment to increase capacity at the station in 1932. As space was a problem, due to no cheap land being available, two platforms of 750 ft and two of 550ft were constructed in an island format. The entrances and exits were also streamlined at this time.

The late 1950's saw electrification in the form of overhead lines. The first trains to run along this were in November 1961, with a full electric service running from June 1962.

In the 1980's, the trainshed roof was demolished to make way for office space to be built above (in much the same way as Charing Cross and Cannon Street have been developed). A new entrance was put in Coopers Row, which gives direct access to the platforms and is a quicker route to the underground station and DLR station at Tower Hill and Tower Hill Gateway respectively.

One other item of note in this history section is that Fenchurch Street is one of only two termini in London not to have had a dedicated station hotel built (the other being Waterloo). However due to its proximity to the City, there were plenty of hotels to choose from a short distance away, and this probably dissuaded the various train companies from ever contemplating building one.

The railway station in 2020

Fenchurch street is unique as it does not have direct access to the London Underground. Instead the nearest Underground stations are at Aldgate (Circle or Metropolitan) or Tower Hill (Circle or District). For this reason, I have not included an Underground station section in this walkthrough. However a walk to Tower Hill Underground station is recommended if you have the time, if only for the views towards the Tower of London.

But if you have arrived from said stations, it is just a short walk to Fenchurch Place where the station is located. It is placed at the end of a rather pleasant semi-circular roadway. The elegant façade of the station building contrasts starkly with the surrounding glass fronted hi-rise buildings. Most of the roadway around the station is given up for Taxi ranks, and a few bars and bistros are scattered within a minutes walking distance.

Moving up to the building, a clock sits centrally at the top of the building, nestled within a very nice arched roof. Below, a grand canopy covers the path directly in front of the entrances to the lower half of the station concourse. The middle doorway has a British Rail symbol, with a Network Rail sign beneath which has Fenchurch Street Station written on it. Whether this will be replaced is to be seen, as the station is now owned by the current train operating company 'C2C', who run all services to and from here.

At time of writing the doors are wooden and blue in colour, with British Rail symbols put on the glass with stickers. As you enter the doorway, on your left is a fast food outlet, and to the right a retail outlet. Two escalators and a set of stairs will take you to the upper concourse, but do not do this just yet.

Move towards the left and enter a small corridor (a small departure board is also above your head here before you enter the corridor). Ahead you will see on your left the lifts to the first floor. Also here there is a small retail outlet to your right, and then access to the toilet facilities. You will also see a set of stairs to the first floor as well if you go towards the toilet entrance. Tiles of cream and brown adorn the walls, the ceiling is low and it is lit with fluorescent lighting.

Turn back towards the entrance, and then proceed to go up the escalators, which have more cream and brown tiling. At the top of the escalator and straight ahead you will see the gatelines for all platforms. However, to continue this tour, turn to the left, go past the  stairwell, then turn left again. Above you is signage for the set of stairs and the lift which lead down to the toilets we saw earlier. Moving further forward some payphones are on your left and the main ticketing office is in front of you.

As you turn again to your left you will go past some retail outlets and a public house is nestled in the corner. Keep turning left and seating will be on your left, with further retail to your right. As you may have guessed, you have now done a circuit around the escalators you came up on! Once you re-enter the mini concourse, take a second to look up at the ceiling. It looks early 1980's in style, with lots of square 'pyramid' looking fluorescent lighting. This is quite a low ceiling too, and there is no outdoor light at all permeating the concourse. However the area is uncluttered, with only a small information stand around three quarters of the way to the gatelines.

As you head towards the platforms, a travel information centre is on your left, and further on the left are a set of cash machines. Near to the gatelines on the right is the station office, in what seems to be a temporary structure, perhaps this will change after 2020. Beside this are automated ticketing machines. Above the gatelines are a comprehensive set of electronic departure and arrivals boards. Further on from these in the centre is a large tv screen, mainly used for advertising.

If you are arriving onto the platforms, note that there are stairs down near the end of the platforms, which bring you out to an entrance at coopers row. From here it is a short walk to either Tower Hill underground station or the DLR station at Tower Gateway. This tends to relieve the main entrance at peak times. Also if you can, take the time to go to the end of the platforms where good views of the tracks away from the station can be had.

In conclusion

All in all, this station serves its purpose. However, to be objective, the welcoming exterior with its fine arch and clock unfortunately seem to get left behind once you enter the station. After that it is a mix of 1960's style tiling on the lower floor, which is completely forgotten once you go upstairs where you are confronted with exceptionally clean lines and a 1970's/80's space age feel because of that ceiling! That being said, Fenchurch Street still has its charm, and the relative quiet setting outside the station with the coffee shops, and of course the fantastic views of that frontage, far outweigh the negatives.

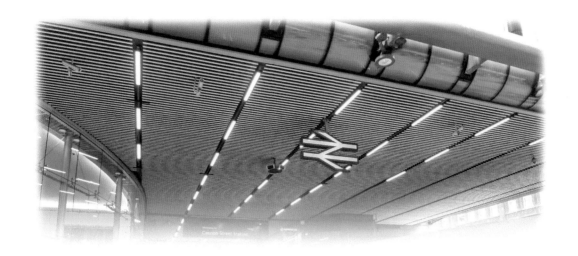

Cannon Street

Opened : *1866*
Platforms : *7*
Underground Lines : *Circle, District*
Current TOC : *Southeastern*
Entry and exit figures 2018/2019 : *20,614,904*

Cannon Street is a true commuter station, mainly quiet between 10am and 4pm, but a hive of activity during the morning and evening peak times. Located in the city district, it is within easy reach of the Bank of England and Lloyds of London.

No wonder then it is the station of choice for high paid professionals who are living in the counties of Kent or Sussex (that is unless their employer has not relocated to Canary Wharf, some 3 miles east!). On the surface, the modern station is a practical people mover. But if you take your time, some real gems from the station's past can be found.

A brief history

Construction commenced in 1863 by the South Eastern Railway Company, from a design by Sir John Hawkshaw. The station is served by a triangular junction to the south of the river, connecting with Charing Cross and London Bridge. The approach to the station is made over the river Thames by an 80ft wide bridge. The length of the bridge is 706ft, supported by four piers. On this bridge only five lines ran, which fanned out on both sides of the river, with the four lines becoming nine as they entered the station which then served five platforms.

The engine shed roof was an impressive 190ft wide, with a central lantern that in itself was 22ft wide and practically ran the length of the shed at 680ft. Two towers designed by J. W. Barry mark the entrance to the station from the river. They are plain at the bottom, but are adorned on the top by a square domed roof and spire. The east tower was found to contain a large water tank during restoration in 1986. This could either have been for replenishing the locomotives, or for powering the stations hydraulic lift systems.

A railway hotel adorned the front of the building, and it had turrets at each end mirroring that of the towers on the bridge end. It was one of the smallest station hotels in London at only five stories high, and like most of them didn't fare very well in the early 1900's. It unfortunately closed for customers in 1931.

On 1st September 1866, Cannon Street Station finally opened to the public. The southern "Triangle" was put to good use providing a 7 minute shuttle service to Charing Cross. This enabled the city workers to gain access to the West End easily. With the shuttles initially leaving around every 20 minutes (it was reduced to every 10 minutes due to popularity); it was far quicker than a 35 minute walk. However, in the 1870's the District Railway opened between Blackfriars and later Mansion House, which proved to be even quicker.

Despite this, Cannon Street became ever more popular, so much so that the bridge was widened to 120ft to allow a further 5 tracks to be added. This now enabled the total number of platforms to be increased by the end of the 1800's to nine platforms.

From 1918, the decision was made to close Cannon Street from Saturday Afternoon through to early Monday morning. This was due to little or no passengers using the station, as most used Charing Cross as it was much closer to the West End. This arrangement stood until 2015, when a new timetable from SouthEastern trains brought a permanent timetabled service back to Cannon Street 7 days a week.

In 1926, electrification was completed on platforms 1 to 5 and one platform was removed. This left platforms 6, 7 and 8 unelectrified for the use of steam traffic. More electrification came in 1929, which left only platform 8 as the only sole steam platform.

During the Second World War, the trainshed roof was extensively damaged by an air raid in 1941. Although much of the iron structure remained intact, engineers deemed it too damaged to be re-glazed. It therefore remained as a skeleton structure, until it was demolished during re-modelling in 1958. This remodelling totally changed the look of the building, there was even talk of a helipad on the new roof, but this was dismissed on noise grounds. During this time, another platform was removed, leaving the current seven platforms which we see today.

The new office complex, which part replaced the roof and former hotel building, was derided by critics. "Bland and totally uninteresting" is how some saw it. It certainly was not as grand an entrance as the Hotel had been. In the 1980's new laws meant that British Rail could effectively "sell" the air over the land which they owned. Hence two office blocks were constructed over the platforms, held up by a huge 6000 ton metal frame. The block nearest the bridge slightly protrudes from the towers, and is known as the Riverside building. This block even has a roof garden. All this means is that if you are walking down cannon street, the station seems hidden behind all these glass facades, totally at odds with most (but not all) of London's termini.

The railway station in 2020

Approaching the station along Cannon Street, you are greeted with what appears a normal 21st century office block. Hung from this are two British Rail signs, one for each of the two entrances. As you face the entrance, take the right hand side steps to enter the station. At the top, there hangs a Network Rail "Welcome to Cannon Street Station" sign in blue.

Immediately to your right is an entrance to the Underground station. However this just a flight of steps. If you need a lift, these can be found if you look to your far left. Of course this entrance is really only of use if you are entering the station via the platforms. For this reason, there is another street level entrance to the Underground, and this will be detailed later.

Looking around, the low ceiling which is clad in silver makes you feel rather penned in. It is very modern in its appearance, the fluorescent style lighting in bright white making it feel almost clinical. Cream tiled floors and grey borders greet your feet, much like a department store. It really is at this point a collection of straight lines, very practical if not very atmospheric. Moving forward, to the right is a coffee shop, an ATM and then the ticket office. Beside this are the toilet facilities, and ahead of you are the gatelines for platforms 4-7.

Turning to your left and opposite the ticket office is a statue called "The Plumbers Apprentice". Produced by sculptor Martin Jennings, it was dedicated in 2011 to commemorate 400 years since a royal charter was issued to the Worshipful Company of Plumbers, the hall of which stood on the site of Cannon Street, until it was demolished to make way for the station in 1863.

Carrying on forward now past the statue (this should now be on

your right), an overhead departure board leads us into the central section of the concourse. Looking to the right, you will see a few electronic ticket machines here before you get to the gatelines for platforms 1-3. If you look behind you, there is a retail outlet, as well as various advertising boards. Going straight ahead past the gatelines on your right, you will see another retail store ahead of you, and to the right of that a pub/restaurant, which is right next to the platform one entrance.

Turn to the left and face towards the exit of the building, and then move towards the steps. Look right, and beside a coffee shop, you will see the lifts which take you to the underground. Above the steps is a large screen displaying adverts, as well as directions telling you what is to be found left and right once you exit the station.

However, if you have an onward ticket do not leave the station just yet. Yes, this a modern station at this point, but if you can, please now gain access to the platforms using the gatelines which are now behind you. For the purpose of this book, we will enter and go down Platform one.

Going through the gateline, look up and notice the clock above your head. This is a flip clock, originally put in in the 1980's by Network South East, the region of British Rail which ran what is now the SouthEastern Railway network. Although now free of the Network South East colour branding, it still sports its original yellow surround. There are more than one of these on the platforms at Cannon Street, and is quite nostalgic to still hear their rhythmic ticking. Also note the central pillars along the platforms, at the bottom of these are still the red, grey and blue branding of Network South East.

Heading up platform one, to the left is the lost property office, followed by a door leading to the station office. Ahead of you the station opens out until you eventually get outside and onto the bridge section. Great views of the Shard slightly to your left, and turning fully left a good view of Tower Bridge and HMS Belfast. Turning 180 degrees gives you another view over the river towards Southwark, Blackfriars and Waterloo bridge respectively. The large tower of the Tate Modern can also be seen to the left of you this side of the bridge.

But the real gem to be seen here is obviously the two towers which provide an impressive entrance to the station. As the only remaining elements of the original station, they stand proud against the skyline. The new office block does provide a real juxtaposition to these fine yellow brickwork pillars, and it is great to see that the importance of these were not lost on the 1980's planners. They can also be clearly seen from the two adjacent bridges, London and Southwark.

Turning away from these, the tracks move further onto the bridge and then fan out making a left turn out of sight towards the triangle going east towards London Bridge and Kent. There is however one line which tracks to the right towards Blackfriars and Charing Cross, a hangover from previous times and no longer a timetabled route, except if needed due to engineering works.

The underground station

Like most of the primarily commuter orientated termini, Cannon Street underground station is quite plain and is easy to navigate. Firstly, let us go back to the underground entrance we went past at the beginning of the walkthrough, the one on the right as you came up the steps from street level. Stairs here will take you down three flights of stairs to a small concourse area. Signage tells you that tickets and trains are to your right.

After turning right at the bottom of the steps, move forwards into the ticketing hall and you will see an exit to your left. This is the alternative route into the Underground station at Dowgate Hill. The gatelines to the District and Circle lines are to be found on your right. A small retail unit is also down here at time of writing.

In conclusion

Cannon Street is very much what you would expect from a commuter station. Although trains now run throughout the whole week, it comes to life during the weekday rush hours. Its large staircases down to street level enable a good throughput of people at these times, and the small but practical underground concourse and station are well equipped to deal with these volumes of passengers. The Station does feels very clinical, with the stark interior roof and bright lighting. But if people could just take a few minutes looking around, they will find fascinating objects such as the plumbers statue, the towers on the platform side, or indeed the nods to Network South East on the platforms.

Charing Cross Station

Charing Cross

Opened : *1864*
Platforms : *6*
Underground Lines : *Bakerloo, Northern (Charing Cross branch)*
Current TOC : *Southeastern*
Entry and exit figures 2018/2019 : *30,235,856*

Charing Cross, a gateway to the theatre district and the Embankment. This small to medium sized terminus sees many visitors and commuters alike, eager to get to work or see that theatre performance. It is within walking distance of Covent Garden, and if you take the short walk to Embankment Underground station, the number of underground lines increases to four.

However the station and its immediate surroundings have an interesting past, one which involves not only the railway, but which also goes back as far as the late 13th Century. As such, it does have an interesting story to tell and some fascinating areas to explore.

A brief history

Before we delve into the history of the railway station, some note must be made about the history of the site and its immediate surroundings. The name 'Charing' can be traced back to the Anglo Saxon word 'Cerring'. This means 'bend' and can be associated to the bend in the River Thames at this point.

The cross element comes from the late 13th Century. After King Edwards I wife, Elinor, died, the King had 12 commemorative crosses built in honour of her. These were placed along the route taken down to London from Lincoln, where rest stops were made. The final resting place for Elinor was in the hamlet of 'Charing', just south of where Trafalgar Square is today.

The cross erected here was the largest and most ornate of the 12. However it was destroyed in the 17th Century during the English civil war. The point where it stood was used to erect a new statue of King Charles I. This is still at that site today, and the point where both the original cross and the new statue sits is still used as the official centre point of London in regard to measurements.

The replica cross outside Charing Cross station was built in 1865, and is larger than the original at 70ft. It was restored in 2009 and is a fantastic structure to look at as you approach the station from the Strand.

Regarding the station itself, it was the South Eastern Railway (who already had London Bridge) who were keen to build a station that catered for the passenger who wanted the West End. It also was very keen to have a slice of the continental travellers market, which was currently mainly served by the London, Chatham and Dover railway at Victoria (and later Blackfriars).

By 1858, Charing Cross was being looked at as the preferred location for this new terminus. By building it here, the company would be able to tap into the lucrative middle and upper class market. Setting up a new company called 'The Charing Cross Railway Company' they put a bill to Parliament, and this was passed in 1859.

Work started on constructing the approach, which would require 190 brick arches and two iron viaducts to keep the railway level. One of the viaducts went over borough market, and the railway paid to have the market rebuilt after construction.

The line slightly inclined as it approached the river, and it crossed it via a lattice girder bridge. This had four running lines across it, and work was completed in 1863. The station opened in 1864 to Greenwich and mid Kent, and fully opened in April of that year to North Kent. Shortly after the station opened, the Charing Cross Railway Company was absorbed into the South Eastern Railway.

The station and its trainshed were designed by Sir John Hawkshaw. At 510 ft long, with a 164ft span arched roof, the design was amazing seeing as it was such a compact space. The design was pretty much replicated in 1866 for Cannon Street station just along the river, giving the two stations a sort of symmetry.

The Charing Cross Hotel was built at the front of the station overlooking the Strand. A large and imposing structure, it contained 250 bedrooms. It was styled to the renaissance period, much like the hotel at St Pancras, but with a more compact look. The architect, Edward Barry, also had a 'replica' of the Elinor Cross made, and this stood in front of the hotel. Although not a true replication of the original, Barry made it as close as he could, bearing in mind only three drawings of the original had survived.

In 1905, during maintenance of the trainshed roof, a large noise was heard by one of the workers. It was soon apparent that the roof was starting to sag, and an immediate evacuation occurred. Some twelve minutes after the initial sound was heard, 70ft of the roof collapsed, pushing out some of the retaining walls with it. Six people lost their lives, including three on the 3:50pm train bound for Hastings which was buried in the rubble.

Although not all of the roof came down, it was decided that the structure be completely removed and replaced. A new furrow type roof was erected above the station concourse which now was not single span, and the roof over the platforms was replaced with a concrete pad where an office block was placed. A huge coat of arms with the letters SE CR was placed at the end of this roof facing the bridge. This coat of arms is currently still there today.

The station was out of action at this time, but fortuitously this enabled construction of the Underground station to go ahead unhindered. Given only six weeks to dig a shaft and make good the concourse, construction on the Underground station started with frantic pace. Amazingly all works were completed on time, enabling Charing Cross to open on time in March 1906.

Like most of the southern rail network, electrification came in stages during the 1920's and 1930's. It was also at this time that the platforms were lengthened to up to at least 750ft.

During the Second World War, the station was damaged on more than one occasion, but it was the night of 16th April 1941 which saw the most damage. The station and hotel were damaged by both fire and explosion, with three trains set alight in the station and a further one on the bridge. A land mine had also landed on the bridge, and the fire brigade positioned hoses to prevent the fires reaching it. Much bravery was displayed that night and the fire station officer as well as the station officer both received the George medal for their efforts.

The hotel needed extensive repair, but this was not carried out until after the war. The hotel had another story added to it during this repair, but this was not in the original style. The two styles clashed until extensive cleaning was carried out on the exterior in the 1960's, when it looked less obvious due to the whole building looking clean.

In 1975 the booking hall was modernised, and not much has changed since. The last major works on the station were in 1986, when work started on a redevelopment above the platforms. An office and shopping complex were approved, which necessitated the removal of the 1906 roof. The retaining walls however are still in use. The work was completed in 1990, with a mixture of office space in the upper floors and restaurants beneath (not accessible within the station concourse). The angular design of this building is quite distinctive when looking at it from the end of the platforms, although as previously noted the coat of arms is still present.

A major change in timetabling came in May 2018, when trains from Gillingham in Kent ceased. Thus anyone wishing to get a train to Charing Cross from the Medway Towns would have to travel to Gravesend and change, or take the new Thameslink service to London Bridge (although this is a 'slow' service).

The railway station in 2020

Entering the station from the Strand, you will see the replica 'Elinor Cross' standing proudly at the Strand end of the taxi loop. It really is worth taking the time to have a look at this structure. It has so many intricate carvings and dominates the entrance. Something else to see however is on the left hand side entrance gates.

Here you can find two plaques, one installed in 1988 and one in 2017. The one at the top from 1988 is a dedication to the readers of the Evening Standard newspaper. They raised funds to plant English Oak trees in London to replace some of the 250,000 lost in the great storm of 1987, one of which is planted at the station. This plaque was erected one year after the storm. The bottom plaque is dedicated to Angus McGill, who initiated the appeal, and was a columnist and cartoonist for the Evening Standard. This plaque was unveiled 30 years to the day after the storm.

At the other gateway, a metal pole displays the British Rail symbol on a cube at the top (at a slight angle), with the London Underground roundel in the middle cube, and a Network Rail branding cube at the bottom.

Looking towards the main station building, the old hotel façade still rises above the main entrance, and the hotel is still in use. The building is in particularly good order, and this can be attributed to the current owners upkeep. A taxi rank is situated within a u shaped courtyard. A subway leads to the underground slightly to the left of the central entrance to the main concourse. This central entrance has retail outlets on the side as you walk through, but we will go through the entrance on the far right.

This entrance is rather ornate, with two columns on top of which sits a bridge like arch. Look up and you will see some ornate carvings at the top of each pillar and inset in the base of the arch. They are painted silver and gold with the cross of St George in the middle. Walking under the arch you will see the concourse ahead of you, and a clear Network Rail plaque situated on the wall at the entrance on the right.

Keep walking ahead, and retail units will be on your left and right. After a short time you will be on the concourse. Looking up here you will see the roof which was rebuilt after the 1905 collapse. As previously mentioned, this dates from 1915, and is still in relatively good condition. The glass was replaced in 1999, and this ensures natural light floods the passenger area, and because of this and the height of the roof, this small space actually seems quite large.

Directly ahead is the entrance for platforms 5 and 6, with a departure and arrival board above. To the front left is the information booth. Turn to your left and you will see the indoor entrance to the underground station. A sign over this entrance also informs you that this will take you via a subway to Strand North, Trafalgar Square and Covent Garden.

As we face the underground entrance, looking right you will see ticketing windows and ticket machines, as well as a little bit of metal seating. Look above the ticket windows and the station clock can be seen, fixed beneath a very pleasant balcony. The windows you see above the balcony are part of the hotel bar.

Of note under the clock there are two plaques, not easy to photograph, and the top one not easy to read. The top is black with white writing and commemorates the stations re-opening in 1989 by the Lord Mayor of Westminster, Councillor Simon Mabey.

The lower plaque, on what seems to be bronze, is a commemorative plaque detailing the arrival at Charing Cross in December 1918 of the President of the USA. He was welcomed by King George the fifth, in order to facilitate better unity between the two countries. A procession then occurred through London, which included crowds lined with servicemen and women, and also an aerial display.

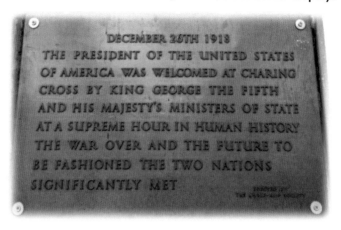

Once you have looked at these, walk past the clock and to your left is another exit to the taxi rank, further on is the entrance to the toilets, and finally another exit to the taxi rank and Strand. Retail units are in front of you. Turn to your right and the entrance to platforms 1-4 will be ahead of you. Above the gateline is an extensive departure board with digital 'flip style' clock.

Go forward a little toward the gatelines, and on your right will be a small waiting room and this contains USB charging stations for your electronic devices. A mural on the wall in here commemorates the 150th anniversary of the station. Next to the waiting room is a place to get drinking water. Take a moment here, if you can, to turn around and look at the roof again. It is not the most ornate in the London termini, but given its age and the fact that it has not succumbed to radical redevelopment it is still a commanding structure. The overall effect is of a Victorian greenhouse, and its regular pattern is very appealing.

If you have a valid ticket to travel and are able to gain access to the platforms, you will, after a short walk, be out in the open. Notice the original 'Network South East' digital clocks as you move down the platforms. Once out in the open, turn back and look towards the station. You will see the modern, albeit art deco styled, office building above the platforms. Although not as historic as say, the towers at Cannon Street, this does give quite a striking impression.

At the base of the office block in the middle right sits the original coat of arms mentioned in the history section. This is quite large and is nice to see that the heritage of the station has not been lost. Either side of the coat of arms are the letters S and R. Looking around you, views can also be had of the London Eye, as well as various other office blocks and buildings.

The underground station

There are many entrances to the underground station here, but as many people travelling by train into Charing Cross will use the one inside the station, we shall also visit that entrance first.

The entrance is to your left, if you have come from the gatelines to the national rail platforms. Going down a set of steps which have orange and cream / beige tiling, you will come out to a small underground concourse area. Turn right and ticket machines will be here, as well as access to the gatelines if you look under a big blue sign. Signage here is good, probably as this is one of the main underground stations for the theatre district.

Carrying on without going through the gatelines will give you access to a set of corridors which are well signposted. Some take you up onto the Strand, and one set even takes you most of the way to Covent Garden. However, in my experience it would be wise to travel in a group if you are traversing these tunnels, they can be quite intimidating if you are on your own, particularly at night.

The best part of the underground here though is to be found on the platforms of the Northern Line. Here on the walls of the platform are huge black and white murals. They depict the history of the construction of the cross (as seen outside the station) and are by the artist David Gentleman. Possibly one of the most striking pieces of artwork on any Underground platform, they are probably rushed past by the majority, but do command a better look if you have the time.

Let us go up to street level, and outside the railway station building for a moment, using the exit on the far right of the concourse this time. You will see immediately to your left an entrance to the Underground. However if you turn to your right and go out of the taxi rank you will see another entrance to Charing Cross Underground station at the top of a hill.

If you look down this hill you will see another underground entrance, some 400 yards away. This is not Charing Cross Underground station, however. This is in fact the entrance to Embankment station. This is where you can catch the Circle and District lines. Thus technically there are four tube lines at Charing Cross, but only two (Bakerloo and Northern) which are actually attached to the station.

Many people will use both to reach Charing Cross railway station, as the walk between them is short, and although you can take a Northern line train to embankment, it would be far quicker to walk between the two (unless, of course you are already on the Northern line!!)

In conclusion

Charing Cross has had a fair few changes in the services which run into it during its lifespan. Once a direct train could be taken between the Medway Towns to here, but the Thameslink project stopped that in the 2010's. It still remains a busy place throughout the day, but especially at evenings due to its proximity to the West End theatre district.

It also has a rich history, with the replica Elinor Cross outside, and this history is told through an elaborate Mural on the Underground Northern line platform. A small station by modern termini standards, but still a particularly important cog in the transportation system in London. And if you look carefully, some architectural gems can still be found.

Kings Cross

Opened : *1852*
Platforms : *12*
Underground Lines : *Victoria, Piccadilly, Northern, Circle, Metropolitan, Hammersmith & City*
Current TOC's : *London North Eastern Railway, Hull Trains, Grand Central, Great Northern, Thameslink*
Entry and exit figures 2018/2019 : *34,645,924*

Kings Cross has been Immortalised the world over as the starting point for "The Hogwarts Express" from the Harry Potter books, by JK Rowling. However, the station also stands proud as the destination and starting point off another famous rail journey, that of "The Flying Scotsman", which connects London and Edinburgh within five hours.

Although for much of its existence busier than its neighbour, St Pancras, its overall façade and purpose of the station was functional rather than fanciful. That is until a major refurbishment in the early 2000's brought a fresh modern feel, while still retaining its character.

A brief history

The Great Northern Railway owes a lot to the Cubitt family. Sir Walter Cubitt and his son were the builder and engineer of the line respectively. Given that the railway was seen as a fast and practical way to go north up the east side of England and on to Edinburgh, an efficient station was needed in London. "A practical station for a practical railway" is how the solution was seen, and so Lewis Cubitt, their nephew, was asked to design such a station.

His design was indeed simple; two 100ft roof spans across the platforms, held by a centre brick column, would create a simple but study trainshed. The front of the building would be a large yellow brick structure with a clock tower in the centre (albeit much smaller than St Pancras' across the road).

The clock itself was installed with bass, tenor and treble bells, enabling the clock to strike on the quarter hours, as well as on the hour. It was sourced from The Great Exhibition in Hyde Park. Its owner, a Mr E.J. Dent, sold it to the GNR at a cost of £200. (Rumour has it that the St Pancras' and Kings Cross clock towers were never to be seen showing the same time.)

Included in this functional façade were two arches, mimicking the trainshed roofs. These were put either side of the clock tower, glazed with smaller rectangular panes of glass. The trainshed had two arched roofs both 800ft long and 105ft wide. They have a maximum height of 71ft above rail height at their centre point.

The concourse contained a refreshment room, as well as waiting rooms for 1st and 2nd class passengers. There was no waiting room for third class passengers, but as there was initially only one train a day accommodating this class it did not seem to matter. A ticketing office and parcels office completed the passenger facilities. All this meant was at the time of opening in 1852, Kings Cross was the largest railway station in Britain.

The railway left and entered the station via a set of tunnels, one under a nearby gasworks. Eventually one tunnel would not be enough, and two more would be built between 1878 and 1882. Known as 'The Copenhagen tunnels' they carried two tracks each bore. The configuration was that 'up' traffic used the eastern bore, 'down' the central bore and goods traffic the western bore. This continued until the 1970's when a remodel closed the western bore as the goods yard was now closed. It is however still used as a roadway for access.

In 1854 a hotel was built by Cubitt's brother, Thomas, to the side right side on a curve alongside a road. It was named "The Great Northern", and although anywhere else it would have been striking, but it was soon to be dwarfed by the hotel across the way at St Pancras.

The square outside the station became known as "the African village". This was because it quickly became inhabited with various stalls, a mail office, excursion office and cab shelter. It was so disorganised, and many said it had a look of a 'shabby shanty town'. Amazingly this continued until the early 1970's, when British Rail would erect a modern ticket office, shops and waiting area, which had the unfortunate effect of masking the majority of the stations façade.

By the late 1800's, Kings Cross would be handling around 250 train movements a day, a huge amount considering the tight infrastructure. Two new platforms were built in 1893, as well as an extensive footbridge which connected all platforms within the station.

When the Great Northern Railway was incorporated into the London and North Eastern Railway in 1923, the station began to prioritise the long distance services to Scotland and North of England. The premier of these was 'Flying Scotsman', starting in May 1928 and offering a direct train service on the 400 mile route. It would depart each morning pulled by a Pacific Locomotive. Others would follow, such as the 'Silver Jubilee' which ran non-stop to Newcastle.

It would, however, be on 3rd July 1938 that the Station would see a record breaker. 'Mallard', an A4 class locomotive, arrived after a run down the East Coast which saw the train reach a speed of 126mph. This still remains the fastest ever speed achieved by a steam locomotive, and is unlikely to be beaten.

During the Second World War, a large section of roof was blown out in May 1941. This wrecked most of the booking hall, as well as some of the general offices. However a temporary booking facility was erected and there was not much in the way of a reduction in services. The roof was eventually repaired in 1946, after much discussion on whether to repair or replace the structure. Also at this time the clock bells were removed and melted down.

Nothing much happened at Kings Cross (apart from the aforementioned new booking hall out the front) until a terrible tragedy struck the Underground station in 1987. Thirty one people died and almost 100 injured when a fire broke out on the escalator from the Piccadilly line. Investigations pointed to a possibility it was caused by a lit match dropped by a passenger on the escalator. The build-up of grease caught fire, and very quickly this fire took hold on the old wooden structure. A flash of flame eventually shot upwards and into the booking hall, setting that ablaze.

As a consequence, all wooden escalators would be replaced on the network, and extensive regulation changes, including a no smoking policy were implemented. The underground station was refurbished with new escalators, heat detectors and sprinkler systems.

The next major refurbishment would be completed in 2009, a radical design by John McAslan. The brief given to him was to create a new ticket office, with a large concourse and eating areas. The new area sits to the west and parallel to the original building, which can be seen from inside the concourse. A huge, white fan like structure rises from the floor, giving this concourse a unique and spectacular roof. Lights are projected onto this white structure throughout the day, making it very dynamic.

Finally a mezzanine level was introduced which contains cafes and restaurants, while various retail outlets are beneath. Access to the Underground station is also available within this new area. A new platform next to York Way was opened in May 2010. It has a quirk as no diesel locomotives can use it due to the pollution risk to the residents of York Way.

The outside courtyard has been tidied up, and the 1970's booking hall removed enabling the full Cubitt façade to be seen once again. It is a fantastic transformation, and one which should help Kings Cross become a station of stature once again.

The railway station in 2020

Starting this tour outside in the courtyard known as Kings Cross square in front of the Cubitt Façade, you can look up and see the yellow stone frontage with the two huge arched windows. The clock tower is very prominent, and overall this is a striking frontage to the station. Take a moment to look around the courtyard. At the time of writing there is a piece by Henry Moore which is on loan from the Henry Moore Foundation.

There are various seating areas dotted around, as well as a couple of refreshment outlets. A good view of the St Pancras Hotel can also be seen here to your left (if you are looking directly at the façade).   All in all this is a nice clean meeting place, and certainly an improvement over its previous incarnations.

The doors you see in the building are now used mainly by exiting passengers from the mainline platforms. This was where the 1970's black booking hall was located, and also was the home to the original booking hall.

Move towards the station traveling to your left as you go. You will head towards a glass Underground entrance. Beside the steps of this entrance is a blue plaque on the wall dedicated to Lewis Cubitt, the stations architect. Once you have viewed this, turn around and head back past these stairs, and once past them turn to your right. The Great Northern Hotel should be straight ahead of you.

Move towards this, but turn right again once past the glass walls of the Underground staircase. You will see the new entrance to the station in front of you now, so move towards this. Above this entrance of is a sort of metal tube lattice with glass over the top. The words 'Kings Cross' are above the entrance with the British Rail logo, and curiously at time of writing, motifs of birds in blue.

As you walk into the main concourse you will of course notice in the distance the huge metal fan coming out of the floor and extending over the entire concourse to form the fantastic roof. But we will come back to that a little later. First look to your right, where through the brickwork are entrances to platforms 0 to 8 (yes Kings Cross has a platform 0). Above these entrances is a substantial arrivals and departure board.

To continue turn to your left though, and you should be facing some automatic ticketing machines which are placed by one of the supporting columns. You should now start walking round a curve. On your left is a bar, which is part of the hotel. Various seating points are on your right, as well as some retail outlets, a payphone stand and a bit further in a set of escalators up to the mezzanine.

Carry on walking along the curve though and you will come to another entrance which will take you out to St Pancras if you cross the road. This area is primarily glass, and echoes the white roof structure throughout. With the views over to St Pancras it is a very pleasant area indeed, and as a contemporary structure it works very well. Of note on your right as you move into this space, is a small staircase. Between two retail outlets, this will also take you up to the mezzanine level, and is pretty well hidden away so is not normally busy.

As we progress further round past this glass entrance, a set of steps will eventually be ahead of you which take you down into the Underground station. It is here that we will turn to the right and head down a wide passageway, past some retail outlets either side and back out on to the main concourse.

When you get there, you will see the reasoning behind taking this route, as directly ahead you will see the start of the white lattice fan, rising majestically from the floor to fill the roof. It is such a superb piece of engineering, and works perfectly in juxtaposition with the original Cubitt station building behind. As previously noted, colour projection is sometimes used during the day, but it really comes alive after dark. Make sure you look up to really appreciate it.

Move towards the structure, but all the while a little to the left. Behind the structure is a substantial ticketing office. As you move to the left, you will see another large arrival and departure board fixed above some retail outlets and cash machines. This board also has two television screens either side of it, mostly showing advertising and news, although it can also be used to inform of upcoming engineering works.

As you walk forwards towards the cash machines, an information point is in the centre of the concourse, as well as other small kiosks. Turn towards the main information point and carry on walking. The arrival / departure board should now be on your right, with yet more retail and eating places to your left, situated under the mezzanine. Walk past the information desk and again try to look up at the roof structure at this point, as it will begin to descend to just past the extreme left of the arrival departure board.

You will soon pass beneath a walkway (more on this later) and will see ahead of you some gatelines. These are for platforms 9-11, and are the 'local' services platforms. To the right of these are some stairs taking you up to a public house restaurant called "The Parcel Yard". Underneath that on the left is the left luggage office, and to the right of the stairs a small walkway which will take you to the public toilets.

At the foot of these stairs turn around and you will see on your left the Harry Potter shop and the photo opportunity for platform 9 ¾. This is always a busy place, so if you wish to have your photo taken make sure you get here with plenty of time to spare. Of note here is that the shop is exceedingly small, so also take that into consideration.

Let us however turn to our right, and walk towards another exit (platforms 9-11 should be on your right as you now walk). This is another small exit that will take you over to St Pancras. A small coffee kiosk is to the left of this exit. As you get here, do not exit, but turn to your left and you will see a set of escalators a little way in front of you. Go towards these and take them upstairs to the mezzanine.

At the top you will see various eating places along the walkway, but its best at this moment to go to the railing just to your left. Great views over the concourse here but of course the view of the roof here just steals the show. You get such an excellent view of the lattice work here, a great photo if you can grab it. However an even better one can be had if you turn to your left and head towards the other elevated walkway that we passed beneath earlier.

If you head out onto this walkway bridge, you will get a nice view down the concourse, with the arrival departure board at the same height of you to your left. If you were to continue along this bridge, as you enter the brick archway, a doorway on you immediate right will be for the first class lounge. At time of writing this is for LNER passengers. And, if you continue further, there are a set of gatelines which will allow you access to platforms 0-8, which give a great view over said platforms. If you can gain access here, you will not be disappointed with the views you can get of the original Cubitt station.

Now head back to the mezzanine and go back down the escalators. Turn to your right and head towards the cash machines beneath the large arrivals board. Between these, and another entrance to the LNER first class lounge, can be found an oval plaque. On it are inscribed words from a poem by Philip Larkin called "The Whitsun Weddings". It recalls a train journey on a Saturday afternoon in the mid 1950's. The same extract can be found under his statue at Hull Paragon Station.

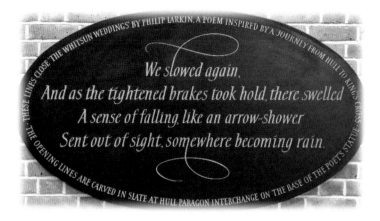

'THESE LINES CLOSE 'THE WHITSUN WEDDINGS' BY PHILIP LARKIN, A POEM INSPIRED BY A JOURNEY FROM HULL TO KING'S CROSS

We slowed again,
And as the tightened brakes took hold, there swelled
A sense of falling, like an arrow-shower
Sent out of sight, somewhere becoming rain.

'THE OPENING LINES ARE CARVED IN SLATE AT HULL PARAGON INTERCHANGE ON THE BASE OF THE POET'S STATUE

Now keep walking back down the concourse toward the fan, until you get to the first brick pillar on your left. At time of writing you will see a stone plaque, dedicated to the re-opening of the station in 2017 by Justine Greening, hung upon it.

If you carry on past this and past the ticket office on your left, you will see a statue and plaque. This statue is of Sir Nigel Gresley, the Chief mechanical engineer on the Great Northern and London and North Eastern Railway, and was created by Hazel Reeves. His most famous designs were that of "Flying Scotsman" and "Mallard". The plaque and statue are in fantastic condition, and are obviously of pride to the station staff.

You will now be at the point where to your left, you will see gatelines to platforms 0 through 8. The next items are unfortunately only able to be viewed past these gatelines, so if you have a ticket (or have been able to get permission), go through and head to the wall to the right of the exit gatelines which open onto Kings Cross Square. Here is where you will find the war memorial. It is a very unusual design.

The names are presented on 11 tall rectangle pillars, lit from beneath. Usually there are wreaths at the bottom of these. To the left hand side of these is a plaque, turned 90 degrees away from the pillars, which the details the memorial and how the current placing of it came about. Certainly a unique take on a war memorial, but the names are legible, and the space given to them is commendable.

Also of note here, down platform 8, is a blue English Heritage plaque. This commemorates the fact the Sir Nigel Gresley had his offices here between 1923 and 1941.

It is at this point where I would normally take you to the Underground station, but as this station is twinned with St Pancras in that regard, the walkthrough of this is undertaken in that section of this book.

In conclusion

Kings Cross station is a great mix of two great architectural delights. Cubits original stone building with its arches reflecting the trainshed beyond is an exceptionally fine structure. But so is the new concourse with that elaborate fan ceiling and open space. It is truly a great transformation and use of space that was already there, without destroying the beauty of the original.

Look around and many treats can be found, as well as places to just sit and admire the station. It shows that with a little effort from both modern architects and historic preservation societies, a compromise can be made to suit everyone. I just hope that this effort continues with any future expansions or renovations to other London termini.

St Pancras International

Opened : *1868*
Platforms : *15*
Underground Lines : *Victoria, Piccadilly, Northern, Circle, Metropolitan, Hammersmith & City*
Current TOC's : *Eurostar, East Midlands Trains, Southeastern, Thameslink*
Entry and exit figures 2018/2019 : *35,984,204 (domestic only)*

The saying "Phoenix from the flames" can rightly be said about St Pancras International. In 2020, it is a bustling hive of culture, with stunningly restored architecture. But its fate was nearly oh so different 60 years ago. Facing closure and the bulldozer, campaigners first saved it, and then the Eurotunnel project regenerated it, into one of the most spectacular of London's termini.

A brief history

The Midland Railway was desperate to have a glorious station in central London. It had run trains into Kings Cross via a partnership with the Great Northern Railway, but always saw this a temporary measure. Thus in 1863, when a bill was passed to construct a railway between London and Bedford, the Midland Railway seized its chance to run its services into a purpose-built station between Kings Cross and Euston. It was to be known as St Pancras, after the parish it was built in.

The railway company commissioned its chief architect, William Barlow, to create a practical and dramatic structure for the trainshed. The design he came up with was radical and unique. A single span arch, 245 ft wide, spanning all five tracks entering the station, anchored using girders at station level. At the time of the grand opening in 1868, it was the biggest single span roof in the world. At its highest point it rises to 100 ft and is 689 ft long.

Since the lines into the station had to cross the Union Canal, the station platforms would be 20ft above ground level. It was initially conceived that the void left would be used to contain the spoil from the excavations, but due to land being so expensive in London, a new use was found. The void would be mainly used to store beer barrels, primarily from Burton, which would arrive from the north on the train network. The Vaults, as they came to be known, would also be used for storing other freight related items. A goods depot was built adjacent to the station in 1887, and this site is where the British Library now stands.

The station was not to be the only impressive structure built though. The Midland Railway also wanted a suitably grand hotel to sit alongside its flagship station. They enlisted the help of Sir George Gilbert Scott to design a lavish and unique building unlike any other in the surrounding area. The hotel he came up with is now recognised as the face of St Pancras.

This truly was a design on a grand and exuberant scale. The inspiration was taken from European buildings. The main clock tower and entrance lend themselves to the architecture of Italy and Belgium, and within the rest of the building can be seen influences from France and Ireland. The overall impression is of neo-gothic style, far away from the Victorian designs which surrounded it. Today, with all that European influence, it seems suitably placed alongside the International rail terminal.

However, for all its glorious looks, the hotel never seemed to turn much of a profit. Kings Cross and Euston had more passengers and consequently their hotels were busier. It closed in 1935, where upon it was used as sleeping quarters for train crews, and later as offices for the British Rail Catering division.

The First World War would see St Pancras suffer greatly, when on the 17th February 1918 it was hit by five German bombs dropped by a huge biplane. This attack killed twenty one people, with countless others injured. However the station still remained operational, even though there was extensive damage to both the booking hall and first class waiting area.

Turbulent times in the 1960's almost lead to the demolition of St Pancras. Many campaigns by eminent historians and conservationists such as Nikolaus Pevsner and John Betjeman helped stave off the bulldozers. This was further bolstered by public opinion, whose disgust at the demolition of the Euston Station arch in 1961, possibly dissuaded the government and British Rail to alienate any more voters and passengers. Eventually the station was given grade 1 listed status, but this did little to halt the decline in the structure.

A turning point came in 1994, when the government confirmed that St Pancras would become the terminus for the Channel Tunnel high speed line, HS1 (although Waterloo would be home to Eurostar services from 1994 to 2007 whilst HS1 was fully built and St Pancras renovated). In 2001, the project to renovate and restore St Pancras began. The trainshed roof was lovingly restored and given a resplendent coat of blue paint. A modern extension of the trainshed roof was built to accommodate the trains to the midlands, and a further one built for the HS1 high speed rail service to Kent.

The beer vault was converted into a modern shopping arcade, enabling the public to see this area of the station for the first time. Overall, this restoration cost in the region of £800 million. The project was filmed by the BBC, and broadcast in November 2007 under the name "The Eight Hundred Million Railway Station".

The hotel was not forgotten within this turnaround in fortune. International hotel chain Marriott, together with developer Manhattan Lofts, gained planning permission in 2005 to fully restore and extend the hotel. It opened in 2011, now named "The Renaissance", a fitting title for the troubled building. With this, the extraordinary and superb St Pancras International Station was fully restored, ready to welcome not only national, but international visitors to London.

The railway station in 2020

This walking tour will start at the glass entrance to the station in Pancras road, directly opposite Kings' Cross. Before we start, just a note that this station is quite vast, and there is a bit of walking involved in order to see all that it has to offer. But please stick with it, as personally I think the effort is worth it to see one of the best preserved stations in London.

Let us walk into St Pancras from here, through an impressive all glass structure attached to the historic building. First, we encounter a light and very airy area. Looking straight ahead at this point you can see straight through to the other entrance at Midland road. The concourse at this point is accentuated by a very high ceiling, giving a great feeling of space, however further in the ceiling is lower. Immediately to the right is a lift which will either take you up to the Southeastern high speed platforms, or down to the Underground station pedestrian tunnels. To the left an escalator and set of steps also take people down to the Underground.

Continue straight on here towards a coffee shop and turn. You will eventually get to a further set of escalators and stairs on your right, with a new pub style restaurant ahead of you. One set of escalators takes you down to the Underground, while two sets of escalators either side of this will take you up to the SouthEastern High speed platforms. If you take one of these escalators up, immediately ahead at the top you will see some coloured benches. These are made from the Olympic Rings which hung at the rear of the old trainshed during the London 2012 Olympic games. If you then turn around 180 degrees, you will find the 4 platforms for the SouthEastern high speed trains. These enter St Pancras under the new trainshed roof, but if you look around you can get a fairly good view of the original trainshed from here, as well as the Eurostar platforms.

Now leave this level by going back down the escalator. Once at the bottom, turn left and take the slight bend to the right ahead of you. This will take you past food outlets to your left and other retail to your right.

Eventually another retail unit will be ahead of you. Turning right here will take you down a corridor for lost property, toilet facilities and the Station Office. Turning left however will take you back down towards the main concourse area via other eating retailers on your left and right. The departure and arrivals board should be directly ahead of you. This is a unique board, coloured blue and stretches around 70% of the concourse area, with information about all the rail companies' services within St Pancras displayed. Underneath this board are other various retail outlets.

Turn right and continue onwards towards the Midland road exit. You will soon have on your right National Rail enquiries and ticket offices. In the middle of this part of the concourse there are also various automated ticketing machines. As we come to the end, to the right are the entrances to the Thameslink platforms.

These are located down a further set of escalators running in a tunnel beneath the station. This 'core' makes travel possible through London to stations to the south (including Gatwick Airport) and Bedfordshire to the north (including Luton Airport). A new service started in 2018 which included a stopping service through north Kent to Rainham (Kent). The platforms here are labelled A and B, and services travel through nearly every 5 minutes at least during peak times.

To the left of you however is the entrance into the new Barrel Vaults concourse area. This was part of the major re-development of St Pancras in the early 2000's and is an impressive area of mainly high to mid-range shops. Currently retailers such as Hamleys toy store, John Lewis, Calvin Kline and even a Nespresso store to name a few are here. Many ATM machines are in the middle of this concourse, attached to the lifts and escalators which take you upstairs to access the East Midlands trains platforms. Take time to look up and see the vastness of the original trainshed, it is truly spectacular, but more on that in a moment.

As we carry on down the vaults, pay attention to the pianos which are placed at intervals in the centre of the aisles. Anyone can sit down and play, and a few famous pianists have been known to stop the crowds with impromptu performances.

Around three quarters of the way down this area on the left is the entrance to the Eurostar terminal, with its associated passport and baggage checks. Another entrance / exit to St Pancras is also here, which takes you back out onto Pancras road. Carrying down the arcade, a set of stairs leads up to a level where you get a really good look at the original restored trainshed in all its glory, so go up these stairs, taking you to an area known as "The Grand Terrace".

When you reach the top of the stairs, you will immediately see a statue to Sir John Betjeman. He is looking upwards, and is a fitting tribute to a man who wrote and devoted a lot of his time to the railways. In fact, it practically makes you look up to appreciate the trainshed, and as you turn back towards the staircase, it literally unfolds in front of your eyes. The sheer scale of the roof structure, without a centre column support, is magnificent. The supports to your right at the side are clearly marked with the makers, the Butterley company, and date 1867. Looking closer at the supports near the ceiling edge, the makers mark can also be seen, together with ornate roundels accenting the fine steel structure.

Turn towards the rear of the trainshed and move forwards towards a brick structure with windows, this is the rear façade of the Hotel. Some rooms even look out onto the station. In front of this is a magnificent clock, which can be clearly read even at the other end of the platforms. Many conceptual art pieces have hung forward and below of the clock, such as the aforementioned Olympic rings.

During 2018 a structure by Tracey Emin was installed here. A simple message "I Want My Time With You", written in her own hand, blazing in pink neon. This was part of a commission by the Royal Academy called "Terrace Wires", which has been running pretty much every year since the Olympic rings were removed.

Below the clock, and to the left of a coffee bar, is another sculpture, "The Meeting Place" by Paul Day. Although some critics did not like it, it is loved by the of visitors to the station, many of whom choose to have a photo next to it. Together with the Terrace Wires installations, it can be clearly seen from the Eurostar platforms in front of it. Standing at a height of 30ft it is very impressive, but take time to look at the base, where various castings showcase the history of the railway. From the bustling underground station scene, to ones of construction and demonstration. The next set of photographs show the sculpture with a few of the base castings.

Paul Day – 'The Meeting Place'

As you turn 180 degrees from the sculpture, glass fronted barriers enable a great view of the Eurostar platforms, the only way to see these unless you are lucky enough to be travelling on a Eurostar train. Again, take a little time to take in the enormity of this space, do not forget that the roof is 100ft at the highest point!

As we turn back towards the statue of Sir John Betjeman, the building in front bears the title "Booking Office", although now it is a bar. It is a credit to everyone involved that even though many retailers have taken over these spaces, It has been done so sympathetically with little of the garish logos or signage of the new occupiers to be seen. On the wall here is a small black plaque which list the dates of the two World Wars with the words 'Hotel and Goods Yards' beneath. Also, along the many pillars, inscriptions pertaining to the Butterley company can be found at many of the bases. Carrying on down the trainshed, halfway down on the right is a champagne bar, which is quite popular.

More retailers and coffee shops are found to our left before we come to the ticket gates for the trains, run currently by East Midlands Trains. It is also here that the original trainshed ends, and the new one begins. It is a real shame that this takes on a box shape, and its stark modern look clashes with the original ornate style. However, on a practical note, it would have cost millions to have extended the look of the original and perhaps would have meant cost cutting on the renovations elsewhere.

It is here we can take an escalator back down to the barrel vault level. Walk forwards, going back past the Eurostar terminal on your left and carry on to the end of this concourse, and through a set of huge doors. It is here we enter the London Underground part of the station, and you are met with a silver roundel, and a plaque which commemorates the opening of High Speed One in November 2007.

HIGH SPEED 1

BRITAIN'S FIRST HIGH-SPEED RAILWAY

THIS STONE COMMEMORATES THE OFFICIAL OPENING
OF HIGH-SPEED 1 AND ST. PANCRAS INTERNATIONAL
BY HER MAJESTY THE QUEEN ACCOMPANIED BY
HIS ROYAL HIGHNESS THE DUKE OF EDINBURGH
ON 6TH NOVEMBER 2007

If you wish to explore the Underground station now, skip to the next section which will take you on a tour of this vast area. If however you wish to continue with just the station tour, continue reading.

Turn back around and go back though the vault, up to the end and turn right towards where we started at the glass entrance. Go through this and you will see Kings Cross Station across the road. Turn to your right and follow the St Pancras station building so that it is on your right. Keep going until you see an entrance to your right. This will lead you back into the station via the Eurostar terminal. Do not fully enter here but look at the two plaques set just inside the lobby.

One plaque is to commemorate the opening of the station by the Midland Railway Company, the other commemorates the 20th anniversary of the channel tunnel and high speed railway services to Europe. After viewing these, move out of this entrance way, turn right and keep heading up the road.

You will see an Underground roundel in front of you, but just before you get to it on your right you will find a water fountain. Recently restored in 2018 to full working order, it is inscribed in memory of Captain Robert Hansler, and was originally erected in May 1877 in association with his widow. A nice place to fill your water bottle, and is probably walked past by the thousands of people who use this road every day.

Carry on walking, and when you get to the Underground roundel, turn to your right and look up at the sign above that reads "St Pancras". This is one of the more elegant entrances and is not used as much these days.

Go up the steps and you will see the Station Hotel in front of you. The impressive clock tower rises high above you and the grandeur of the whole building is evident, It has been used by many film and television companies as a backdrop to St Pancras, even though it is not the station building. Indeed, it stars several times in the Harry Potter films, most notably in the second movie as the Weasleys car takes off over it.

The best way to photograph this is to cross Euston road to the other side. From there many views of not only the hotel, but also St Pancras and Kings Cross, and many a great set of photos can be had from here. Of note as you walk along this side of the road, there is another entrance to the Underground station, emphasizing again what a warren of tunnels awaits you as you get to the Underground Station section. To continue with the underground station part of the tour, you will need to get back into St Pancras via the glass entrance in Pancras Road, head to and through the vault shopping complex to the big set of doors with the silver roundel on it we saw a short time earlier.

This leads us into the most complex underground stations on the network, and I shall attempt to take you through it now.

The underground station

Before we start, just a note that this Underground Station is shared with Kings Cross, and as such multiple entrance and exits to it exist. It is a true labyrinth of corridors and hardly used passageways, which I will try to navigate you through. Also due to the shared nature, we will only take this tour in this section and will not repeat it in the Kings Cross chapter of this book.

As you go through the doors, you will see an information centre on the right. Stop at the information centre, to your left is a set of stairs that go down. If you were to continue going ahead and turn left, you will find exits along this corridor to your right taking you into Euston road. However let us go down the flight of steps on your left.

To the right of you at the bottom are automated ticketing booths. Going past them and again on your right are the gatelines and access to the Central, Metropolitan and Hammersmith and City lines. Carry on down this corridor towards a set of steps.

As you arrive at the steps, a corridor will appear on your right. On the wall of this corridor is a plaque dedicated to the lives lost in the Kings Cross fire disaster which occurred in November 1987. Thirty one people died and one hundred were injured in this terrible disaster, which ultimately lead to the withdrawal of all wooden escalators on the London Underground network, as well as numerous other safety improvements.

If you were to go down this corridor, you will pass under Euston road, and will be either able to exit via another corridor on your left or right. This is a good place to exit if you want an iconic photo of the St Pancras station hotel which will be across the road in front of you (also a good photo of the facade of Kings Cross can be gained by exiting here). If you have taken this corridor, come back in the same way and continue with this mini tour.

Here you will see a small concourse with ticketing machines, and access via gatelines to the Victoria, Piccadilly and Northern lines. Also a big staircase is alongside these (if you come out of the corridor in the previous paragraph, turn to your right and the staircase is in front of you). Going up here will take you to the arched entrance of Kings Cross Station.

Going back now to the gatelines for the Victoria, Piccadilly and Northern lines so that they are on your right and the ticketing machines are on your left, go down the corridor in front of you (not the two we took earlier!!). A little way down here on your right is another exit into Kings Cross Station. Carry on down the corridor though, it is on a slight decline, and retail units are on your left. At the end you will be in the Northern ticket hall. An escalator is in the right hand corner here, some days I have seen it moving down into this hall, other times it has been going up into Kings Cross Station.

In this ticking hall are automatic ticketing machines to your right, and gatelines to the Victoria, Piccadilly and Northern lines on the left. Moving on through this area, you will see a set of stairs going up to Kings Cross Station, and a large silver plaque greets you on this staircase inscribed with the station name and British Rail Logo.

Before we continue, if you have a valid ticket for the underground and can do so, go through the gatelines and at the bottom of the first set of escalators turn to your left (towards Piccadilly and Victoria lines). Follow this corridor all the way to the gateline for the Victoria line but continue on. You will now be going through a small corridor, this is the exit to Pentonville road, and a very unique mural by Badry Mostafa containing both the British Rail and Underground Roundel can be found at the end of it.

At time of writing, this exit is only open Monday to Friday 0700 – 2000 , and not at weekends. An interesting note is that this used to also be the entrance to King Cross Thameslink Station, but now this is closed, and Thameslink services currently go via the platforms at St Pancras.

Going back to the mini tour, you will see a piano on your left by a pillar. Ahead of this on a slight right is another long corridor. Go down this and you will see sets of escalators and stairs going up. Halfway down on your right is a walkway with rainbow coloured lights along it. This will take you to Granary Square, and because of its unusual nature is quite well photographed.

Turning back into the main corridor, going up the set of escalators or stairs in front of you (or the lift on the extreme right) will take you back to the big glass frontage of St Pancras where the main tour started, and where this tour of the Underground station will finish.

In conclusion

St Pancras International is a superb station to visit. The cosmopolitan feel and vast open spaces make it a pleasant place to explore. The trainshed roof, best viewed from 'The Grand Terrace', is also a great place to sit and watch the world go by. Perhaps you will find a seat at one of the many of the café's and bars on offer and just people watch.

The underground station, although confusing at first, can offer interesting corners and corridors, many of which end in a surprise or two. All in all, St Pancras International is a fitting gateway to the United Kingdom, and one which we should all be proud of.

Paddington Station

Paddington

Opened : *1854*
Platforms : *14*
Underground Lines : *Bakerloo, Circle, Hammersmith & City, District (Wimbledon – Edgeware Road)*
Current TOC's : *Great Western Railway, Tfl Rail, (also the 'Heathrow Express Operating Company' who operate the 'Heathrow Express' in conjunction with GWR)*
Entry and exit figures 2018/2019 : *38,181,588*

Paddington station is a grand beginning to any railway journey. Designed by Isambard Kingdom Brunel, it is a marvel of 19th Century engineering. The trainshed roof, which lets in copious amounts of light, dominates the interior skyline, and the station benefits from a roomy concourse area.

As well as Brunel , its other famous 'visitor' was the Michael Bond character 'Paddington Bear', which is celebrated in the station with not only a statue but also a dedicated shop. The station has seen many improvements over its history, and now has a particularly good retail and food space behind the concourse. As a gateway to the south west of England, it has stood the test of time and quite rightly sits amongst the great railway stations of Great Britain.

A brief history

The story of Paddington station starts in 1832 with four Bristol businessmen who wanted a railway built between Bristol and London. They put out a request for applications and stated that they would only accept the cheapest. However this did not stop Isambard Kingdom Brunel from submitting a plan which would not be the cheapest, but it would be the best. They obviously liked it, as he was chosen to be the chief engineer of the line in 1835.

Many sites were considered for the London terminus, including one which ended at Euston Square. Brunel allegedly did not like this idea of a shared station, and was therefore pleased when the idea was shelved in 1835.

The station therefore was to be built in the west of the capital, by the Paddington branch of the great Union canal. However this first station was not of the grandeur which Brunel wanted. It was mainly of timber construction, the passenger facilities being under the arches of a bridge in Bishops road. However it has a place in history as the terminus in which Queen Victoria completed her first railway journey, from Slough to London, in 1842.

Eventually in 1850, work began on the site of the current Paddington station. Brunel designed it, but employed another architect, Matthew Wyatt, to provide the decoration.

The station is situated in a cutting, and therefore much of its grand look is contained within the station. Brunel wanted it to have the look of the Hyde Park 'Crystal Palace', and so an iron and glass roof was imagined with decorative work provided by Wyatt. Three arches with a combined width of 240 feet and length of 700 feet covered the platforms. The centre span of these three has a width of 102 feet, with a total height of 54 feet.

A Suite of rooms were built especially for the Royal family, and office buildings were positioned alongside the platforms. The old boardroom windows can still be seen, above the Charles Jagger war memorial on Platform 1. It is styled in a Venetian way, and is a credit to the station owners down the years that it remains unchanged and in good condition. With all this ornate work, It is no surprise that the building work took four years. However in 1854, the first train left from the new terminus.

As a side note here, the Great Western Railway was built to Brunel's 'Broad Gauge' specification, so the platforms were further apart than the other London termini. A third rail was eventually introduced to help facilitate both broad and standard gauge locomotives, and the last broad gauge train left Paddington in 1892.

A hotel was built at the front of the station, the first of the large scale 'railway' hotels to be built for a London terminus. However unlike many, it was a separate concern, although it was Brunel that wished it to be built. Positioned on land previously used for shunting, it had a look of a French Chateau. It boasted an impressive 103 bedrooms plus reading, billiard and smoking rooms. Family bedrooms could also be found, and the overall feel was to attract only the best clients. It opened in 1854, and still operates today, and at time of writing it is part of the Hilton group.

Another first for the station was that it was the first Underground London terminus, as the Metropolitan line ran to Farringdon via a cut and cover railway which left from the Bishops road end. This opened in 1863 and proved to be extremely popular, with 38,000 passengers on opening day.

In 1915, the station had a major enlargement with three new platforms added, covered with a facsimile of Brunel's roof for continuity. Further improvements were completed in 1933, with the installation of luggage lifts, and a superb steel footbridge which linked all the platforms. A ticket office was also put on this bridge above platform 8.

Like other London termini, the station was damaged during the Second World War. In 1941 a bomb damaged a departure side section of the station, and in 1944 another bomb damaged the roof above platforms 6 and 7. But because of the best efforts of railway staff, and the emergency services, Paddington still managed to maintain a pretty good service during this time.

During the late 1950's, all of the suburban services changed from being steam to Diesel Multiple Units. The suburban services had been increasing since the mid 1930's, as many new housing areas were built on the outskirts of London. The last steam service would leave Paddington in Mid-1965, the long haul routes now mainly being served by class 42 and class 52 locomotives. Eventually these would also be replaced in the mid 1970's with the now iconic 'High Speed Train'.

An extensive refurbishment was completed in the 1990's, with the area known as 'the lawn' surrounded by glass, making it an impressive retail and restaurant area with good views of the main concourse.

Recent years have seen a new entrances either built or planned. The entrance at Paddington basin has a fantastic façade, and this will be mentioned and discovered in the walkthrough. Additionally a huge entrance for the station is to be located at new area called Paddington Square, including a dedicated entrance for the Bakerloo line, which will involve pedestrianisation of London Street. This new area will include a ticket hall nearly 4 times the size of the existing one, making the Underground experience much less cramped. The project was due for completion in 2022, although as with many major projects this may slip due to the 2020 Covid-19 pandemic.

Additional to this is the fact that Paddington will be a station on the brand new Elizabeth line, linking it with the east of London. The new line has, however, had a well-documented delayed opening timetable. Originally planned to open in December 2018, at time of writing the line was due to start running trains on this new line from Paddington to Reading by August 2020.

The railway station in 2020

Many people will get to Paddington by the London Underground, but as the station has a vast array of underground station entrances and exits, picking one to start with would be difficult. For that reason, I have decided to start the walkthrough via the street entrance at Praed Street. Here, there is an entrance to an Underground station on your right, before you descend the road towards the arched entrance.

And what an entrance. The archway above with the elegant iron work behind glass leads the eye into the trainshed roof beyond. A coat of arms for the Great Western Railway adorns the top of the arch, which totally juxtapositions the lettering underneath the arch for Paddington station. This lettering seems a bit 'stuck on', but I suppose practical in telling you the station name.

As we enter onto the main concourse a royal mail post box is to our right. The superb canopy now unfolds above us, and natural light floods the station. The effect of space is evident straight away, this building certainly does not give you a claustrophobic feeling. Note the white pillars to your left, accented with black at the top slipping down the length of the trainshed. The very ornate arches are also part painted in black, and the whole thing is a great feat of engineering and symmetry.

Move slightly forward and then turn to your right, so that you head towards a sign which directs you to platforms 12 through 14, a taxi rank and the left luggage office. As you head under this sign, if you look right, you will see a small entrance to the Bakerloo line. As stated in the history, this entrance will be enhanced with a totally new one once the Paddington Square project is finished. It will certainly open out this exit which can cause a bottleneck at peak times.

As you move past that entrance, a coffee retailer is on your right. Heading further forward the ceiling closes in, and you will see a beige wall ahead of you. Further signage on this wall directs you to the Hammersmith and City and Circle Underground lines, plus the aforementioned platforms and taxi rank. Seating is found a little further forward on your right, with cashpoint machines on the wall in front of you, as well as another food retailer just of the left of them.

You have to turn left at this point, so do so and carry on. You will now be travelling parallel to the platforms on your left. On your right a nice waiting room is to be found, and further on from this the toilets (which being a National Rail station are free) are also on your right. Past that is an automated ticket machine, and above you copious amounts of signage ensure you get to your required destination.

Just past that ticketing machine, take time here to turn to your left and head towards a glass barrier, which gives you a view over the platforms at Paddington. Some good side on views of the trains can be had here. Once you have had a look, turn back and continue down the corridor.

On your right, before a set of stairs, you will see the left luggage office. Do not take these stairs just yet, continue straight down the corridor towards the platforms. The floor opens out slightly as you enter this mini concourse, with the gatelines to Platforms 12-14 ahead of you, and a set of lifts are to be found to your right.

Turn back around and head back to the set of stairs you just saw and go up these. This will take you up to the taxi rank, and the entrance to the Hammersmith and City and Circle Underground lines. As you reach the top, turn left and move under the modern canopy.

Carrying on under the canopy, the taxi rank will be to your right. Eventually you will pass a red arch on your right, and will see a gated area to your left. This is to enable emergency services access to the concourse. Continuing on you will see a big sign above you, directing you either to the Underground station, or to the platforms on your left. Carry as if you are going to the Underground gatelines. Continue walking, and you will soon see a set of stairs to your right, turn and go up these.

At the top you will be presented with a fantastic open area, with the canal straight ahead of you. At the time of writing there is a canal boat just to your left which has a seating area on top and serves teas, coffees and light snacks. I hope this stays here, as it is a great place to stop and catch a drink by the canal.

Turning around back towards the stairs, you will see a large totem, and you will also get a look at the rather impressive glass entrance which we came through up the stairs. This really is a calming place to come if you have the time.

When you are ready, go back down the stairs. You will see maps for the underground lines ahead, very useful if you are wishing to find which underground entrance to use. There is also a Tfl rail map also. Now, turn to your left and carry on walking until you come to a red arch on your left, look to your right and you will see another passageway which heads under the trainshed canopy. Turn and take this passageway.

After a few steps, you will turn slightly to the left as you near the end, and then it opens out slightly. If you kept turning left, you could go down a set of stairs to platform 8 and 9, but we will keep moving forwards, going directly under the trainshed. You will now be on a bridge above the platforms. You will see a metal wall on your left, with a small strip of glass on top, move towards this and look over.

The entire station opens out in front of you with great views over the platforms towards the front entrance and "The Lawn". A closer view of the roof here is possible, and you get to see the supporting pillars in great detail, especially the orate iron work on the sweeping girders. A really good photo opportunity if you can take it.

After looking out over the station, turn back and carry on walking over the bridge. You will see a couple of gatelines on your left as you go down, these enable access to platforms 2-5. On your right you will see various advertising hoardings and above these the end of the arched trainshed roof. You can get views over the platforms as you move down, one of the best is from the stairwell at platform 5.

As you get to the end of this bridge, timetables are on your right, and at the end also on your right is a set of stairs which lead up to company offices. Directly ahead is a lift to take you down to platform level. Before we descend a set of stairs on your left, take a little time to look at some other ornate ironwork on the wall in front of you. Small details like this at Paddington really make this station, and it is great that it has never been removed or covered up.

Let us now go down these stairs and you will find yourself on platform 1. As you move along here, notice how wide the platform is. Coupled with the high roof, it really does evoke a sense of space and freedom. As you go past the office spaces on your right you will eventually come to a statue, designed by Charles Sargeant Jagger This is dedicated to the Great Western Railway men who gave their lives during the First World War.

Two carved images are either side of this monument, the left one a tied rope and anchor, and the other to the right is an eagle with wings spread. A door to some offices is next to the eagle carving with a coat of arms at the top. There is also a door next to the rope and anchor carving, with another coat of arms, this leads to the Great Western Railway offices.

Above the statue are the original bay windows of the Great Western Railway boardroom. With surrounds in olive green, they are quite striking, and easily missed if you are not looking for them.

Carrying on down platform 1, you will pass the first class lounge on your right. Ahead of you, you will see a large clock attached halfway up the wall. There are faces on three sides of it and it is always nice to see these timepieces not only in situ, but also in working order. As a bonus, just after the clock if you look up on your left, are said to be the old station offices for Brunel. But there are two other things to note in this clock area before you look at that.

If you stop and turn to your right, at the time of writing there will be a small alcove with a mural at the back. This is where the entrance to the Elizabeth line should be. At the front of this alcove however is a statue of a bear. Not any old bear, but Paddington Bear. The sculpture was designed by Marcus Cornish.

Paddington Bear is probably what many people think of when they are asked what the station is famous for. The main character in Michael Bonds' books, he is found in the first book by the Brown family at the station, and is taken home with them. A genuinely nice photo opportunity for the little (and not so little) ones.

Only a short walk from the statue, there is also a colourful seat on your right, with a green plaque above giving a brief history of the character, and the fact that the 2014 film 'Paddington' was filmed at the station. The seat was designed by Michelle Heron. Again, a good photo opportunity, especially as you get the chance to 'sit next to' Paddington Bear.

Leaving the seat, turn back and continue back down platform 1. Various eating and retail outlets can be found on your right as you head back towards the front of the station. The station reception can also be found on your right here, almost opposite the buffers. As you continue down you will see on your right a set of brand new toilets, and then the main ticket office.

The vast concourse will now open up in front of you. An arrival and departure board is on your left, and an information point is located directly under these. Carry on past this board, towards the large glass fronted wall. The wall is topped with an ornate white ironwork arch, and is very impressive if you can stand a little back and get an overall view of it.

Past this glass is an area known as 'The Lawn', and contains retail and restaurants. Seating is to be found on your left just before your enter the last set of right hand glass doors into The Lawn.

Upon entering at this point, you are greeted with an escalator and stairs just ahead of you. Lots of seating is in here, and a good selection of retail and eating places can be found, including a rather nice public house at the top of said escalators. In fact, good views across the station and Lawn can be found by going up these escalators, so it is well worth doing so, even if you have no intention of using the retail on the various floors.

If you were to move past these escalators and turned right, you would see an exit from the station. This is known as the 'Horse Arch' entrance at Eastbourne terrace . Re-opened in mid-2020, after the Elizabeth line works were completed, it has an open front with small glass canopy. However at this time though, remain at the bottom of the escalators.

If you look to your far left on the ground floor of 'The Lawn', you will see a dedicated 'Paddington Bear' shop. In here you can buy all sorts of Paddington paraphernalia, books, stuffed toys, even the famous Paddington marmalade! Be sure to stop in here if you need a souvenir of your visit, but be warned you could spend a lot!

After taking time to explore what is on offer in this area, exit back onto the concourse and move towards the entrance to platforms 8 and 9. Go onto the platform area, you won't need a ticket, and carry on down until you come to a statue in the middle of the platform. This is a statue of Isambard Kingdom Brunel, produced by John Doubleday, sitting on a chair holding his infamous hat. He is facing the directors balcony. A very striking piece and another good photo opportunity, especially if there is a train behind it to create a good backdrop.

After you have finished here, exit the platform onto the main concourse once more. Once there, turn slightly right and you will see a set of escalators and stairs in front of The Lawn. These will take you down to the Underground station for the District, Circle and Bakerloo lines. Do not go down these, I will come to that part in the Underground Station section later. To the left of this Underground entrance are escalators that come down from a mezzanine level of The Lawn.

If you were to get to the top of this escalator, you will get a good overview of the concourse. If you decide to go back into 'The Lawn' to get to this area, you will not be disappointed. You will notice from this vantage point the copious amount of freestanding silver information boards scattered over the concourse, as well as various small retail outlets. With this spectacular view over Paddington, this section covering the National Rail station ends.

The underground station

Underground access is by various points around the station, as you have seen when we walked around. Let us start with the entrance which you should be next to if you have followed the walkthrough previously. This entrance goes down via stairs and escalators, under 'The Lawn'. Considering the railway station is very open, this area has quite low ceilings.

The area does begin to open out however, and you will find that retail is on your left and right, with ticketing machines on the left also. Entrance and exit gatelines for the District and Circle lines are slightly straight ahead to your right.

An entrance walkway to the Bakerloo line is here also, but at time of writing is only open at certain parts of the day. As previously said, the new Bakerloo entrance being planned should help relieve areas such as this during peak times.

Coming out of this, up the stairs and back onto the main concourse, walk towards the higher platform numbers past the main station entrance which formed the start of the walkthrough. As you go past this on your right is another, very small entrance just for the Bakerloo line.

Carry on past, and as in the walkthrough, take a left and follow the corridor to the steps which are signed to the taxi rank and the underground. You will be outside once at the top of the steps. Just carry on walking down here, you will eventually pass the entrance to the National Rail station on your left (opposite the red arch). Carry on and you will see the gatelines for the Hammersmith and City, Circle and District lines.

In conclusion

Paddington station, in its Brunel form, has not lost any of it grandeur in its 150 year history. Sympathetic renovations, plus new additions make this termini a joy to travel from. Look closer and hidden gems can be seen, whether that be the impressive structure holding the roof in place, or the original balconies of the station offices. With the Elizabeth line just around the corner, the station will be accessible to more people in the future. A good thing, as this Brunel Masterpiece needs to be seen and explored.

Euston

Opened : *1837*
Platforms : *16*
Underground Lines : *Victoria, Northern (both Bank and Charing Cross branches) **

Current TOC's : *Avanti West Coast, London Northwestern Railway, Caledonian Sleeper, Tfl London Overground*

Entry and exit figures 2018/2019 : *46,146,456*

*this may increase to Circle, Hammersmith and City and Metropolitan lines if a subway is built between Euston and Euston Square

Euston railway station has been the terminus for what is now the west coast mainline for over 180 years. At first taking passengers to and from Birmingham, the station would eventually be a lavish affair, with a tremendous gateway arch and hall to match.

Unfortunately, it suffered greatly from a complete redesign in the early 1960's, making it more like an airline terminal than a railway one. Due to this, prominent conservationists would heavily protest at such a thing happening again to other London Termini.

It has, however, some history available to view if you are prepared to walk and look, and one could say that in its current 2020 state, it stands as a monument to how to make a station functional, but lose its identity.

A brief history

The site occupied by Euston station today was not the original site planned. The London and Birmingham railway had originally thought a site near Islington near the Regents canal would be a more appropriate place, due to its proximity to the docks. Other sites included both a terminus near Marble Arch and one nearer Maiden Lane, near where Kings Cross is now. Eventually however a site at Euston grove was agreed, and construction began in the early 1830's.

At a cost of around £2.5 million, raised by selling shares, the building of the railway to and from Birmingham was an amazing if ambitious achievement. Finding a route which traversed and went around many gradients was challenging, but Robert Louis Stephenson was able to do it, having created the Birmingham to Manchester railway successfully by 1830.

An ambitious railway demanded an elaborate and ambitious station, however on first opening it was quite an ordinary affair. Two platforms were in use to start with, with trains only running as far as Boxmoor, Hertfordshire, until the full route to Birmingham was completed in September 1838.

A basic trainshed roof covered the platforms, and amenities to the traveller were similarly basic. Not that surprising, as this was the second mainline terminus to be built in London and it had only one other to compare to (London Bridge being opened just before Euston, and was in itself a very ordinary looking station as well).

The station did however have one unique aspect. Due to the fact that there was a 1-in-77 incline out of the station, regular steam locomotives of the time were not able to get out without help from a system of ropes. These were pulled by two winding engines located in Camden. Trains coming into the station freewheeled with the aid of a brakesman.

In May 1838, a 72ft high 'Arch' was erected facing out onto Drummond Street, costing around £35,000. This 'Euston Arch' as it would become known, was at a total juxtaposition to the actual plain station building. Some thought it overly extravagant, as it not only was an entrance arch, but had two lodge buildings built adjacent to the main arch, with a room in the roof of the arch itself.

The next buildings to arrive however would be fairly grand. They would be the first two London's great railway hotels. Opened in 1839, and to the front and either side of the arch, they were two four story buildings. The one to the left was called 'Victoria' and was the lower class of the two. The one on the right however, called 'The Euston' was meant for the first class passenger.

The station would eventually be improved after the railway company amalgamated with the Grand Junction and Manchester and Birmingham Railways to form the London and North Western Railway (LNWR) in 1846. New offices, meeting rooms and more importantly a Great Hall was planned for the station.

Thus in 1849, the Great Hall was opened. The designer was Phillip Hardwick and it was built by William Cubitt and company at a cost of £150,000. Entering through one of five doorways, passengers first entered an area with mosaic flooring. Five more entrances would guide them into the Great Hall.

At 125ft long and 61ft wide, it had a curved staircase in stone at the northern end leading to a gallery. Off of this gallery were many offices including board rooms and suites of the company officers. The ceiling of the Grand Hall was highly embellished and had 8 bas-reliefs of either busty women or muscular men, representing the areas of London, Northampton, Carlisle, Lancashire, Liverpool, Birmingham, Chester and Manchester.

The main booking hall was to the east of the hall, and a smaller one to the west of the hall, the latter taking bookings for the Midlands and branch lines only. If you went west facing the main booking hall you would reach the parcels office and further down a place called "The Queens Apartments" (today's equivalent would be the VIP lounge). This area did not last too long though, eventually closing and becoming extra storage to the parcels office.

However, upon leaving this lavish hall, passengers were greeted by a very mundane platform area, totally out of keeping with what came before. A dull first class waiting room (and even worse second class one) awaited the passengers. It really seemed as if all the money for the station had been spent on that lavish Great Hall, with nothing left for the platforms!

Over the remaining years of the 19th Century, various works were carried out on the station, namely the raising of the trainshed roof by six feet. Also, the hotels were joined together in 1880, which totally cut off the view of the arch. A bronze statue of Robert Louis Stephenson was placed in the forecourt, and currently can still be seen there. By 1891 the station had increased its size, and a new VIP room was built to accommodate special passengers, and a 288 lever signal box, at the time the largest.

The next major change would be in 1922 when electric traction was used between Euston and Watford, which required platforms 4,5 and seven to be electrified. In 1927 the Great Hall received a small renovation, with the pillars coated red and the installation of electric light.

The first threat to the original building came in 1933, when a chairman of the railway proposed that a huge rebuild of the station take place, with the Great Hall being a casualty. Plans were drawn up which included a huge hotel and offices on Euston road, which eventually could even accommodate helicopters on the roof! However even after materials were sourced to build the new station, work was slow to start and before it could, World War two broke out.

Damage to the station during the war was limited to the roof and platforms 2 and 3, where a bomb landed in-between them. It was repaired by the newly formed British Rail at a cost of £500,000. Instead of carrying out new plans, they continued with the existing station, putting a train arrival bureau between platforms 1-3 in 1951. The station became the first to issue fully mechanised tickets when 10 machines were installed in 1960.

It would be however the year before that, 1959, that the plans would be laid out once again for the 'improvement' of Euston. Decisions were made that the station be demolished and replaced with a thoroughly modern station. This would also mean the demolition of the arch. It was the latter which would prove to be highly controversial. Many wanted to save it, and thus plans were submitted to move the arch.

The only problem was that of cost. The government were unwilling to pay out the cost of relocation, citing that this would cost £120,000, as opposed to demolition which would only cost £12,000. Meetings between Prime Minister Harold Macmillan, Sir Charles Wheeler (Royal Academy President) and other supporters, including Sir John Betjeman (Victorian Society President) did take place, but to no avail. So in late 1961, Macmillan sanctioned the demolition.

Progress was very swift indeed, and the arch was gone by the end of 1961, despite more protests. However, as is seen in other chapters in this book, other developments to London termini in the 1960's would be changed due to the uproar over the arch.

It would not be until 1968 when the new station would be officially opened. A stark contrast to what had come before, the new building was made of concrete and glass, with an extensive flat roof. The overall look was that of an airport terminal rather than a railway station, and people soon complained of its soulless look. However, the design did meet its brief, the station was able to accommodate many passengers in a smooth efficient manner.

It is said that many architectural developments in the 1960s look very dated now, and Euston station is no exception. Redevelopments to the West Coast mainline during the early 2000's made it an efficient way to get to the North west and Scotland, but apart from that nothing else changed. That is until in the late 2010's, when work started on the new High Speed 2 rail link.

The railway station in 2020

This is a walkthrough of the station as it was in January 2020. Because of the extensive works on the station in readiness for High Speed 2, many objects described here may have been moved or even removed when you are reading it. As such this walkthrough may not be accurate, but it does serve as a snapshot of the station in 2020, something which this book is all about.

That being said we shall start outside the station in the piazza area, immediately next to the opening for the Underground station. This wide courtyard at time of my walkthrough was full of construction fencing as work continued on the initial work for the High Speed 2 reconstruction of Euston, which is happening to the left of this piazza. There is still a bit to see out here, and it does give you a good look at the 1960's station façade.   The Euston sign with the British rail and underground emblems is to your left, both on the building roof and just above the left hand side entrance. The overall look really is that of an airport terminal rather than a railway station.

If we move towards these Euston signs, ahead of you will be the statue to Robert Louis Stephenson, sculpted in 1870 by Baron Carlo Marochetti. At the time of writing there was no plans to move this, but as this was a work in progress anything may have happened to it by the time you read this. It is nonetheless a great statue and nice to see a large monument to such an influential person in the history of UK railways.

After viewing the statue, turn back around and walk towards the underground entrance, you will have a restaurant in front of you on a raised platform. Immediately to the left of this is an entrance to the station, with the word 'Euston' above it as well as the British Rail and Underground signage. Turn towards this entrance, and you will see that the outdoor walkway stretches down on your right. Although we will not go down here, there are a few retail outlets plus a substantial bike rack.

Enter the station here, and you will quickly see that there are steps to your left leading up to a mezzanine level. Ignore these and move into the station; retail units are on your right and eventually you will move into the right hand side of the main concourse. Over to your forward left on the wall is a huge arrivals and departures board. Three large metal signs, one reading 'Euston', one beside that on the right a Network Rail logo, and one beneath which reads 'departures'. are placed on the 'wooden' wall above the board.

Either side of this board are huge screens displaying mainly advertising, but occasionally station and route information, especially if there are planned engineering works in the future. Look up here to see the roof, I could be critical, but it is of its time, and a rather good example of 1960's architecture. The flooring is styled to look like marble, and as a concourse it is one to the least cluttered of all the London termini. Having said that it really is just a 'holding pen' for passengers, many of which wait with suitcase in hand until their service and platform appear on the giant board.

Ok, perhaps I am being too mean. The station is a little lifeless yes, yet it is super practical and efficient. Going further forward you will see many retail outlets, which are placed in between the platform entrances. Looking at the platform entrance in front of you, which should be for platforms 7,6,5 and 4, you will see that it slopes down ahead of you, with no notable barriers.

Many of the platforms are like this, and tickets are checked by hand just before you enter the platforms. There is not much of note if you were to descend these ramps, and the plain look of the station is carried on through to the platforms.

But we shall not go down this set of ramps, instead as you get to their entrances, turn right and go down a corridor which has retail outlets both left and right of you. Entrances to platforms 3 to 1 are here also on your left. The toilets are at the end of this corridor, and as it is a Network Rail station, these are free to use.

Turn back around and head back onto the main concourse. You will see above left and ahead of you the mezzanine level (currently called 'The Food Terrace'), and a set of escalators also to your left. These will take you up there, so take them now. At the top you will see a public house in front of you which wraps around to the side, but first turn around 180°. You should now be facing a lift which will take you down to ground level. To the right of this is the First Class lounge for the West Coast mainline services (at the time of writing this is Avanti West Coast, who took over from Virgin Trains in December 2019).

Turning back around toward the public house, walk towards it then turn right and start to walk along the mezzanine. This area is full of eating and drinking outlets to your left, and seating areas to your right which give good views over the concourse, and more importantly, the departure board. In the middle on your right a set of escalators can be seen which take you back down to concourse level. We shall stay on the mezzanine however and carry on towards the end.

As you get to the end, you will see big glass windows which enable you to look out over the main booking hall area. A quick turn to the left and then right through some doors into a small open area with a little seating. You will see a set of stairs to your left, take these back down to the ground floor.

At time of writing you will see some photo booths ahead of you as you leave the staircase. An exit to Melton Street is to your left, but we will turn right and head down towards the main concourse again. Immediately to your right will be lifts which take you to the mezzanine, and just past those an exit onto the main outdoor piazza, with Stephenson statue visible through the doors. Carry on forward though and after a few yards, turn to your left. The ceiling here is very low with spotlights, and you can feel a little hemmed in at this point.

As you move forward the main ticketing hall will be to your left. This is at contrast to the dark entrance you are in, with high ceilings letting in lots of good light. It is to be seen if this will remain in its current place when the extension of the station is complete, but for now it is one of the more pleasant ticketing halls in any London termini.

If you have gone into the ticketing hall for a look, come out and head into the main concourse area. Do not move to fast at this point though, instead head to the first black pillar you see on the concourse. This is the first plaque of interest at the station, easily missed if you were in a rush. It is dedicated to Lance Corporal John Alexander (Jock) Christie VC. He was a parcels clerk at Euston, and enlisted in 1914 for the First World War. Serving at Gallipoli, he was wounded, but

returned to action in Palestine. His bravery in single-handedly repelling enemy lines resulted in him being awarded the Victoria Cross.

Moving past this plaque and head towards the middle pillar, then onto the next one which is opposite some seating. If you turn to look at this pillar, another plaque is on it. It is honouring Asquith Xavier, who was the first non-white train guard at Euston in 1966. His story is once of triumph over adversity. After initially being refused for a guards job at Euston (he was already working at Marylebone), he persevered and with the help of MP Lena Jeger and Barbara Castle, gained the position. However he continued to be the subject of racial abuse during his time on the railway. He died in 1980 in Chatham, Kent, after 8 years spent in the Medway towns.

After looking at this, walk around the pillar and head back towards the entrances to platforms 7 through 4. At this point turn to your left, and carry on down, past retail units on your right until you get to entrances to platforms 11 through 8. If you were to go down here, not only would you get to the gatelines but would eventually encounter stairs and a hallway which will take you to the Underground station. You may wish to explore this, but afterwards make your way back here to continue.

Going down the corridor again, you will eventually leave the concourse behind, the ceiling being noticeably lower after you do. It was in fact always that low, but the proximity to the open air concourse makes it feel less so. Other entrances to platforms are along here on your right, as well as smaller departure boards near each one.

As you move past platform 15, a coffee retailer will be on your left as well as a cash machine on your right. Further down on your left is the Left luggage office, and opposite that a customer lounge. It is a very nice customer lounge with departure boards, and not that well used as it is tucked away down here. Something to bear in mind if you are early for a train or heavily delayed and want a sit down.

Moving further forward, the corridor narrows further still as you go past the entrance to platform 16. It is here on your left that you will find an entrance for the British transport Police. Carrying on down further will exit you to Melton Street, and it is here that you will also find the Station Office. Go out of here (if you still can) and turn left, then at the end of the building turn left again and head back into the outdoor piazza where the Stephenson statue is. If this is not possible, make your way back to the statue via the main concourse.

Although that is the station building covered, there are one or two other areas of note outside and nearby if you have the time. Move away from the station past the statue and head towards the road which serves as the main bus drop off. This is Euston Grove, and in the centre of it is a memorial to railway personnel who lost their lives during both World Wars. It is very elaborate, and a fitting tribute to these railway workers.

Just slightly forward from this and either side sit two triangular arched blocks. These are in fact the two lodge buildings which were part of the Arch. Within them at time of writing are bars, but that is not the main interest. Around all of the corners are written the names of destinations from London Euston. Much like the stone one at Blackfriars, but this is a much more extensive destination list. A coat of arms adorns each of the corners as well above the names. Although the occupiers are not of that era, at least they are being used, and in turn this means they are preserved for all to see.

Move now towards Euston road, and turn to your left. As you walk down here, you will see a small park to your right. Carry on until you reach the end of this park, which is the intersection of Euston road and A4200 (where the busses exit). Enter the park at this point, and you will see a small plaque by the first tree. This is dedicated to all the public and railway workers who have died on the railway. Although installed in 2001, the plaque is in a terrible state and could do with replacing and installing in a better way rather than just on two thin metal posts.

If you wish you can now travel on foot to see Euston Square Underground station, and a plaque dedicated to Richard Trevithick. I have not included this within the Underground station section due to the fact that this station is, at time of writing, not connected to the mainline station. If you do not wish to do this, or do not have the time, bypass the next few paragraphs, going back to the piazza and stand in front of the Underground entrance.

However to see these, come out of the park and onto Euston road once again. Turn back towards the arched blocks, but when you can, cross over Euston road. Keep moving along the pavement, and past the Wellcome Foundation building (this has a glass frontage) on your left. On its far corner, at the intersection of Euston Road and Gower Street is the entrance to Euston Square Underground station. Here you can get onto the Circle, Hammersmith and City and Metropolitan Lines. Plans are still on the table to join this Underground station with Euston Railway station, and this could be achieved within the High Speed 2 rail link works.

Turn left into, and continue up, Gower Street. You will pass entrances to the University College Hospital on your right, and when you pass an entrance to University College London (a gated entrance with a grassy courtyard) on your left, keep walking and eventually on a white building to your left you will see a large black plaque (opposite is University Street). This is dedicated to the 18th Century engineer Richard Trevithick.

This pioneer of industry is hugely important in the development of the steam engine. Having initially developed the huge beam engines used in the mining industry in Cornwall, eventually his experiments with high pressure steam would lead to him building the world first steam 'locomotive' "The Puffing Devil" in 1801. This is a fairly hidden plaque, but good recognition of an engineer who was an important figure in British industrial history. From here, make your way back to the main Euston station by doing the walk back in reverse, eventually ending up so that you are in the main piazza.

The underground station

Entry to the underground station at Euston from the piazza may be changing, especially as it may soon be linked to Euston Square, but I will nonetheless give a short overview of how it looks at time of writing. Once you enter a small entrance area, you will need to turn left in order to go down a set of escalators. This will take you to the underground station concourse. Straight ahead here are a set of stairs and lift which will take you up to mainline station concourse level.

As you turn into the concourse, you will see the gatelines for the Victoria and both branches of the Northern line, and opposite these ticketing machines. There is however a corridor next to the gatelines which will take you up to the Overground mainlines. This is the entrance/exit at platforms 11 through 8 of the mainline station which we discovered earlier. It has a few retail outlets along its length, and is of quite a reasonable size.

That is about it, it is quite an easy underground station to navigate, but the ease of integration with the overground services via that walkway must take a lot of pressure away from the other entrances to here within the mainline station.

In conclusion

Practical and efficient, but unfortunately dull, explains Euston station at the start of 2020. It stands as a monument to 1960's architectural Britain, although perhaps not in the positive sense. A large chunk of grey concrete, with only the remaining Lodge buildings, Stephenson's statue and a war memorial its current redeeming features.

But Euston station is in the processes of being re-built once again in the 2020's. As the London terminus for the new High Speed 2 rail link, one can only hope that this new station does this terminus justice. Other redevelopments, such as London Bridge have shown that a sleek and efficient modern terminus does not have to be architecturally dull. I am hopeful that this ethos is followed here, and that the station is made not only practical, but also gives it a sense of style and grandeur again.

London Bridge

Opened : *1836*
Platforms : *15*
Underground Lines : *Jubilee, Northern (City Branch)*
Current TOC's : *Southeastern, Southern, Thameslink*
Entry and exit figures 2018/2019 : *61,308,364*

The oldest of the permanent termini, London Bridge is now a super modern hub, suitable for the 21st century. It is full of the modern necessities with clean wide open spaces, but charm can still be found within and around its walls. Its history is vast and complicated, with various railway companies operating to, and even through it, in its lifetime.

One of the combination termini (where trains terminate alongside through services), the station is right in the heart of a financial district rising all around this part of London. This includes the imposing 'Shard', which rises just over 1000 ft above the station.

A brief history

It was in 1831 that a proposed 3 ½ mile railway be constructed between Greenwich and Tooley street. To enable the lines to run in a timely fashion it was proposed to elevate the railway along a viaduct made of 878 brick arches. The lower portions would be rented out to small business. Of note here is that of a public house which was located in an arch halfway along the viaduct. Appropriately named 'The Halfway Inn' (later 'The Railway Tavern'), it was opened in 1850, and remained so until 1967.

The viaduct took around sixty million bricks to build, all of which were made in Sittingbourne, Kent. Trenches twenty four feet deep were needed for this grand structure, with each pillar having a concrete and iron tie support to stop them moving. Additionally, a pedestrian walkway ran alongside the tracks. This enabled residents and visitors great views over London, and a close look at the railway, all for the sum of 1 pence. However, as the railway became more and more popular, this was removed in order to lay a further track.

The line partly opened in February 1836, but only as far as Spar Road, effectively making this station the first station termini in London. This was short lived however as in December 1836 the line eventually ran through to London Bridge station. However, unlike Euston which was to open in the following year, the station was very basic. A three story building (containing a booking office) led to a very simple station where passengers would need to climb steps or go up ramps to get to the two platforms. These platforms were open to the elements; no train shed was provided. A small trainshed was eventually built between 1860 and 1870, but this only extended to halfway along the platforms, and it would be only after the rebuild in the 2000's that individual canopies were erected to run the entire length of the platforms.

Expansion to the routes provided at London Bridge came soon after the 1836 opening. The London and Croydon Railway Company continued the line north in 1839, and between 1840 and 1842 the viaduct was widened to four lines from Corbett's lane to London Bridge. This was for new services from the South Eastern Railway and London and Brighton Railway Companies. The increased traffic facilitated a new station building in 1844, the first of many rebuilds over the next 20 years.

The most notable of these rebuilds came between 1847 and 1850, in which the station was dived in two. The South Eastern Railway took over the northern side of the site, and the newly formed London, Brighton and South coast Railway the south side. These were split by a huge wall, and the two companies enforced their own rules and regulations on their respective halves of the station. This would cause services, especially those of the horse drawn omnibuses, to pay differing charges to both railway companies as they traversed both sides of the station.

This division remained until 1923, when both the southern rail Companies were brought together to form the Southern Railway Company. A footbridge formally linked the two station buildings in 1928, enabling passengers to access all the station easily for the first time in 89 years.

The arches under the station were used in the Second World War as shelters. However as noted in an inspection in October 1940 by the Home Office and health inspectors, conditions were not ideal. It was found that there was only one running tap, and only a few toilets. The floor was just earth, and refuse was seen everywhere. On top of this a further inspection by the metropolitan Police commissioner concluded that the shelters were not strong enough to protect the people inside, and recommended that improvements be made. Unfortunately, however, before any substantial improvements could be made, a bomb hit the shelter in February 1941 and 68 people died with 175 injured.

The station after the war became busy once more, and problems faced by passengers for years occurred again. This was due to the station still being hard to navigate, with peak times becoming a melee of passengers and vehicles, all moving in different directions around the cramped space of the concourse and the overbridge. It desperately needed an overhaul, but this would not occur until the mid-1970's.

When it came, the overhaul would be the most radical remodel since it first opened. The concourse was completely rebuilt with space for retail outlets at its sides, and a new wider overbridge gave more comfortable access to the platforms. As well as this, improvements were made to track signalling, and the track access to Cannon Street and Charing Cross was streamlined to virtually eliminate the bottleneck at Borough Market Junction.

Further improvements came in the late 1980's and early 1990's as the Jubilee underground line was extended eastward towards East London, the area under the platforms being transformed into a booking hall. All of these improvements would pale into insignificance with the advent of the Thameslink programme.

This ambitious one billion pound programme has completely transformed the station. The entire area below the platforms has been opened up into a huge concourse with high ceiling. There are now nine through and six terminating platforms, all of which are accessible via new lifts and escalators, and as previously noted they also have canopies running their entire length. The new station concourse at the lower level is larger than the pitch at Wembley Stadium.

London Bridge has always been a busy peak time station, a hive of activity for the workers of London. Through all the renovations and remodelling's however, one thing has remined constant, the huge viaduct which serves it. A huge feat of engineering which still stands proud above the streets of South London as it makes its way to Greenwich.

The railway station in 2020

I have in this book started many tours from outside the station, but in the case of London Bridge, I feel that many people will enter or leave from the Underground station, so that is where we will start.

After going up the escalators, you will come out into a passageway. This is in fact Joiner Street, and at the time of writing was under refurbishment. To your left is an entrance to Tooley Street, but we will turn right.

Moving down joiner street, follow the station signage to the main station and on your left, you will soon see an area called The Western Arches. Go down here in the direction of the main concourse. Huge pillars surround you on the left and right as you move down, with various retail outlets within the walls. The toilets are to be found around halfway down, on your right.

If it is not too busy, it is a great photo opportunity, as the pillars symmetrically disappear into the distance. You are in fact below the through railway lines at this point, and effectively moving in an easterly direction.

The roof then opens up a little as we cross another major walkway, which is Stanier Street. Turn to your left here and go down the street to see plaques on the wall on your right, showcasing the past and present  development of the station. If you have the time, take a look at them. They are a wealth of information about how the railway lines have come in and out of the station over the past 180 years, as well as great history of the station itself. If you were to carry on going down, you will once again exit onto Tooley street.

Turning back to the arches, carry on back to the intersection in the Western Arches, and face back east again. You will see a few large brick columns with the main station concourse ahead of you. On one of these columns is a railway sleeper, with a dedication to the opening of the new station in 2018 by HRH The Duke of Cambridge. Moving forward you will enter the main lower concourse.

The first thing you should do here is to look up for a second and appreciate how light and airy the station is at this point. The roof is accented with areas of wooden slatted ceilings containing strips of lighting at regular intervals. This creates a warm feeling, and certainly is much better than the stark white or stainless steel ceilings of many other modern mainline stations. Here we will turn right, going past retail outlets on you right and under a huge escalator and set of stairs. Immediately after going under these on your left is the main ticket office, and on your right are one of many lifts to the upper concourse (of more later).

Around three quarters of the way down on your left is a huge departure board. This lists all departures in an A-Z format. Just along from this also on the left are a set of automatic ticketing machines. As we head towards the exit here (which takes you out onto St Thomas' Street), to the right of you near the doors are another set of departure boards, albeit much smaller. To the left of you by the other exit doors is a memorial plaque to the First World War. It commemorates the five thousand six hundred and thirty five members of staff of the railway company which lost their lives during that War.

Just a small side note here : If you go out of the station at this point, you will enter St Thomas' Street. Turn to your left and go down one arch and enter it, you will find the station reception. There is no access to platforms here, so it really is only of use if you work here, or need the reception. If you were to turn right, and go down the road a little, you would eventually reach Joiner Street again, which is where the entrance to the Shard viewing experience is (booking is most defiantly recommend for this). Also here are steps here up to the bus station and upper concourse of the station.

But let us turn back onto the main concourse, and return past the main ticket office to the escalators and steps we passed under a little while earlier. These will take you up to the Bus Station and upper concourse area, so let us go up these to explore.

As you leave the escalator, walk through a small passageway and you will see in the distance the exit to the bus station. This used to be regarded as the main entrance to the station. It is now an all glass fronted affair, very much in keeping with the Shard which can be seen towering above you on your left if you exit at this point. We will not rush through to exit however, but carry on to this upper concourse.

Various departure and arrival boards adorn the sides of the area here, with retail outlets and a few ticketing machines as well. Turning left into the main concourse hall, you will see a large departure board hanging from the glorious glass ceiling.

The roof space here is really impressive, mainly glass, giving lots of natural light for the passengers and staff alike. If you go under this departure board, you will find the gatelines for Platforms 10-15. These are the only terminus platforms here at London Bridge, and at time of writing are served by Southern Railway. If you are travelling from here, once past the gatelines, take a while to admire the new roof structure as it seems to snake away from you. Views down the railway lines here are very impressive, the curvature of the platforms mirrored by the canopy, well worth sneaking a of photo if you can!

One thing to note here is that at time of writing, you cannot access the through platforms from this area. To do this you need to go down to the main concourse and go up from there, so let us turn back to the escalator, and go back down.

At the bottom, turn to your left and carry on down towards the glass frontage ahead of you. As you head down here, various other retail outlets are on your left, with an information point sandwiched between a set of gatelines on your right. You will also see a few escalators which are beyond the gateline, and the roof here is back to the wooden slat ceiling which was seen on the other side of the concourse. Various departure boards are positioned above the retail outlets, you really cannot fault the amount of electronic information about services at this station.

Near the exit, more automated ticket machines are located to the left, and going through the exit will take you into Tooley street. This used to be the location of the London Dungeon, but that has since moved to a site near the London Eye. If you leave via this exit, take a moment to look at the new sweeping lines of the façade. A fantastic piece of new architecture which blends very well with the vastness of the viaduct is on it. This is really all you can see if you do not have a railway ticket or permission to go past a gateline.

However, assuming that you do have a valid ticket, let us go back onto the main concourse, and go through a gateline into the second part of the concourse. The roof really seems to open up as you move into this space. A huge area, with many central but tastefully constructed concrete columns, shaped a bit like egg timers, support the roof and platforms above.

Seating is provided around the circumfrence of these columns. Big, long escalators and stairs take you up to the platforms (arranged in pairs, except platform 1). As well as these, various lifts are dotted around in the middle, making this station very accessible indeed. Departure and arrival boards adorn each side of all the lift shafts, as well as on the 'back' wall near the aforementioned stairs and escalators.

Unlike the upper concourse, access to all the platforms, including the terminating ones, is available here on ground level. More eating places are to be found nestled between the escalators. If you had only visited this station before this rebuild, you will appreciate how much this space has opened up. It really helps the flow of people and feels less like a cattle pen now.

The underground station

There are different ways to enter the underground station, we came into the station using one, and so I will endeavour to provide a small guide to another. Let us discover an entrance which some may use if they have come in via the terminating platforms, or even by bus. This can be reached by exiting the gateline then carrying on straight and going outside, via the big glass exit, into London Bridge street. You will see the bus depot head of you, and to your right a set or archways which hold the through rail lines.

Head towards these arches, and the path will start sweeping to the left. Eventually you will see a sign for the underground under the arches, as well as an information point placed just before them. If you take this entrance, you will go down a set of stairs which will take you to the Tooley Street entrance. At the bottom of the stairs, you will be in the same place that the walking station tour started, just before the Western Arches.

Take a right though into the underground station. Jubilee line gatelines are immediately to your left, with automated ticketing machines to your right. If you carry on forward you will see an exit to a small retail arcade to your left (this will take you back into the far end of Joiner street, near the entrance to the Shard Experience). As you move further forward, you will see a small flight of stairs which either take you to the gatelines of the Northern line to your left, or to an exit to Duke Street Hill to your right.

In conclusion

London Bridge is now a fantastic, open plan London terminus. Gone are the days of a dark and unappealing station, where it felt more like a rabbit warren than a major London transport hub. The roof space is opened up due to the concourse being lowered, and natural light floods the majority of its floorspace.

However, look deeper and you can still see the heritage. The arched walkways that lead to the underground station on the lower concourse are proof of this. And if you step outside on the lower concourse, within a few steps you can see the vast viaducts which enable this railway to snake around this part of the city. It is still a great engineering marvel, and with the investment both on the station and the surrounding area, it should now be a more pleasant experience for the commuter and tourist alike.

London Liverpool Street

Opened : *1874*
Platforms : *18*
Underground Lines : *Central, Circle, Hammersmith and City, Metropolitan*
Current TOC's : *Tfl Rail, Tfl London Overground, Greater Anglia*
Entry and exit figures 2018/2019 : *69,482,532*

Once the busiest railway station in the world, London Liverpool Street has an ornate interior contrasted with its once busy commuter status. People are always shuffling in and out at peak times, probably feeling like sardines. Many, if not all, will not have had the chance to just stand still and admire the architecture around them, as they sped towards either the exits or the platforms.

Although changes have been made in the last 40 years, the superb architecture remains on the concourse, and new links with the Elizabeth Line may eventually make this station one of the busiest the world once again.

A brief history

Built amidst the previous Shoreditch and Bishopsgate station, Liverpool Street was the terminus for the Eastern Counties Railway. Opened in 1874, it had 10 platforms, two of which extended under the station buildings to a junction with the Metropolitan railway. Designed by Edward Wilson, the gothic style design contained the booking offices, as well as the Company offices of the Great Eastern Railway. A trainshed roof made of iron had two small outer spans and two much larger central spans. These covered the ten platforms, of which two were for mainline trains and the rest for suburban services.

The original station buildings were around 90ft high, with a spired clock tower. Various other buildings were attached, especially to the east where more platforms were installed at the Bishopsgate end. A hotel, "The Great Eastern Hotel" was also built and ran down the length of the new frontage.

However, all these expansions created a myriad of entrances, exits, platforms and bridges. Indeed, the main footbridge across the station was not nearly wide enough and was on two levels. It is said that it caused too much confusion for passengers wishing to traverse the station, meaning possible missed connections as a result.

Like many railway companies, many workers were sent to fight in the first world war. A huge marble plaque was erected in the station near the booking hall in 1922 to commemorate the losses of the Great Eastern Railway. This was relocated to its current site near the main entrance in 1990.

Liverpool Street was heavily damaged during the Second World War. A train was wrecked on platform 1, and a bomb which landed on Broad Street viaduct managed to place a wagon on the station roof! Also, many of the buildings were damaged and even the clock tower was burnt through on the inside.

It is, however, what happened before the second World war which Liverpool Street Station is most remembered. Known as the 'Kindertransport" many trains arrived at the station from Harwich, carrying children escaping Nazi Germany. The first arrival of 200 children was on December 2nd 1938. By September 1939, almost 10,000 children would arrive from Germany, Austria, and Czechoslovakia. All would be without their parents; most would never see them again. A statue was unveiled outside the station in Hope square to commemorate this event in 2006, it is called "Kindertransport – The Arrival". Another statue is within the station, and this was dedicated twice, in 2003 and 2011. More on these in the walkthrough.

Through the early 1960's, the station was refurbished by British Rail. A new clock tower was built, the station cleaned and fitted with fluorescent lighting. The booking hall was refitted in 1965 and a post Office installed, although the latter would not prove to be popular and closed in 1968.

With all the refurbishment, it was with surprise that in 1974, British Rail earmarked Liverpool Street (and Broad Street) station buildings for demolition. These were to be replaced by a new underground terminus. Whilst Broad Street did go the way of the bulldozer, campaigns by leading conservationists, including Sir John Betjeman and Spike Milligan gained pace. Due to their efforts and that of public support, Liverpool Street station building was saved.

The plans now included restoration of the trainshed roof, and this was completed in 1984. The main roof was also refurbished, and this completed in 1987. A new subway entrance to Bishopsgate was opened in 1991, and in the same year Queen Elizabeth II officially opened the station. However over £250,000 of damage was caused by the Bishopsgate bomb of 1993, resulting in a two day closure whilst the station was made temporarily safe. An interesting side note is that Liverpool street had the last working 'flapper board' departure board. This was eventually converted to a digital board in 2007.

During Crossrail excavations in 2013, a burial site was located which was attributed to the Bedlam burial ground. Around 3000 interments were found during full scale excavations in 2015, and these were reinterred in Essex.

The railway station in 2020

A complex set of over walkways and corridors await us in Liverpool Street, so let us start the tour of the current station by heading in via the entrance at Hope Square. The main article of note here is the Kindertransport statue which sits just behind the main gates as you go through them.

Called 'Kindertransport – The Arrival', it was created by Frank Meisler and Aire Ovadia, and supported by both the Association of Jewish Refugees (AJR) and World Jewish Relief. A fantastic memorial and well worth spending a couple of minutes to look at.

Above some benches at the back of the square is a commemorative plaque for the dedication of Hope Square. A food retail outlet is also on your right, but we shall move forward towards the class fronted entrance.

Going through the entrance will take you onto the upper mezzanine of the concourse. The fantastic roof structure opens out in front of you, take time to admire the work on the pillars, they are extremely decorative. The ironwork is also detailed as it spreads out from these pillars, and each one is interconnected to form a superb array of coloured struts. The natural light falling onto the concourse is very pleasing indeed.

Ahead there are escalators down onto the concourse, and if you look to your left here are some beautifully restored arched windows, reminiscent to those seen at Kings Cross. Move towards these and carry on down past some seating, on to what seems like a bridge walkway. You will see to your right as you carry on down here a most fantastic view across the concourse, perhaps arguably the best concourse view of any termini in London. Stop when you are halfway across the walkway, and face this view to your right. It gives you a superb panorama of the roof, as well as the many shops and bars which populate the station.

A huge departure board sits equidistant between the concourse floor and the roof, as if suspended in mid-air. A great photo opportunity if you have the chance, especially on a sunny day. One thing to note as well, the glass panels here on the walkway have the London Underground roundel on them.

Turning back to our left, carry on down the walkway, you will eventually see another walkway to your right. Do not turn right here just yet, carry on down the corridor. You will see an exit to the bus station on your left, and the side of some retail units to your right. Eventually you will get to an area on your right which will give you fantastic views over the station platforms.

Although the trainshed roof here is still spectacular, it does seem to be on the dark side. The glass roof has somewhat yellowed it seems, which is a shame. It is still a good photo opportunity, nonetheless. At the end of this corridor is an exit to Sun Street Passage. Do not go out here, instead turn back around and head back into the main building.

Once at the convergence of the two walkways, turn left and go past a parade of retailers on your left, with the main concourse below you on your right. You are now heading towards the departure board, but occasionally look over and down to the concourse and of course up to admire the roof as it unfurls above you. You will see the entrance to the Underground if you look over to your right just before you get to the board.

At the departure board, turn right to go underneath it. Good views can be had of the station both to your left and right over this bridge, so take time to look if you can. As you reach the end of the bridge you will see a plaque on the wall, dedicated to the East Anglians who died during World War One, and was erected by the London Society of East Anglians.

After viewing this, move just around the wall in front of you, and after couple of yards, look left. Above you on the wall you will see the very impressive monument in white marble, noted and seen in the history section. Above this is a stone frieze which reads 'Great Eastern Railway'. This was salvaged from Harwich House, named after the port in Essex which Liverpool Street served. It housed offices for the railway, mainly freight operations, but also for the Sealink brand. The freight company Freightliner was also run from here.

Going back to the memorial, underneath are the individual plaques for Captain Charles Fryatt and Sir Henry Wilson, (seen above), both of whom were decorated in the first world war. To the left of those is the lift down to the main concourse. Below the memorial, it is quite common to see wreaths and other dedications.

After looking at this impressive memorial, walk back along the walkway, towards the arrivals and departures board (which will be on your right) and carry on this walkway toward the other end of the station. On your right are cafes, and indeed the building of the Great Eastern Hotel. Before you get to a big chain public house on your right, look above and to your right. You will see on the wall 3 brick reliefs, one depicting a steam train, above it a ship belonging to the Great Eastern Railway and above that a scene involving coal being put into a steam engine firebox.

Carrying on down the walkway, the next entrance/exit is now in full view. Almost a mirror image to that brick and glass archway design at the other end of the station, it is a very impressive sight, and like most of the station, allows copious amounts of natural light to fill the station. Go through this exit, leading you out to Bishopsgate. The former Great Eastern Hotel building is on your right, and if you enter you can still see the original ceiling of the ballroom.

Keep moving down here until you get to Bishopsgate road, then turn around. You will see a glass canopy with steps and escalators that lead down to the main concourse. Either side of this are two brick columns, one on the right is a clock tower and one on the left with the insignia of the Great Eastern railway.

Look again to your right and you will see an ornate metal totem rising into the sky and on the top a London Underground roundel, with the name Liverpool Street underneath on a ring. This is surely the most unique station totem in London!

Facing towards the main station again, move towards it slightly to the right, walking past the glass canopy and up a small ramp. This will take you to the outdoor bike racks, and gives a good close up view of the glass arches inset into the brickwork. Turn around, go back down the ramp, and turn towards the station. A glass plaque welcoming you to the station is on the pillar to the right. Head through past this pillar and go back in, onto the mezzanine level, this time on the right side of the walkway heading towards the Information board.

To your right as you walk down there is a telephone and an entrance from where the outdoor bike racks were. You will see a public house and restaurant called 'The Parcel Office', there is a small corridor running alongside it on your right, take this corridor and go down to the end for views over the taxi rank and down over the platforms in the distance. You can also see the left luggage office beside the taxi rank. Stairs here will take you down to both if you wish.

Let us, however, turn back towards the mezzanine, looking to your left as you do so at the archways at waist level , which are highly decorated. As you exit the walkway, keep walking forwards and over the bridge to a set of steps on the far side. Go down these steps onto the main concourse.

Right in from of you at the bottom of the steps is a seating area. To make things easier, turn around and head to the far end of the concourse again, where the steps rise up to the Bishopsgate exit. Before you get to them, notice two silver plaques to your right on a brick pillar. These commemorate the station being the winner of the best kept station in London in 1993 and 1996.

After viewing those, turn slightly left and head towards gatelines 15 through 18. Currently as of 2020, some of these platforms are where the TFL Elizabeth line trains were running to Shenfield. The ceiling here is low and covered in fluorescent lighting, and the columns holding this up still bear the Network South East branding at the base.

A small coffee retailer is to your left as you continue towards a white wall with advertising. After the ornate manor of the original roof, this area feels very sterile in nature, almost London Underground-esque. Turn to your right, more seating and some photo booths can be seen on your left as you move down. Curiously as you reach the end of this mini corridor, a set of steps on your left can take you to Bishopsgate East.

Another coffee retailer is ahead of you, now turn right and go down back towards the open air concourse. As you do so, seating is to your right, as well as the stairs up to the Bishopsgate entrance. Also of note before you go through the brick and metal entrance (and by the side of a newspaper retailer) there is (at time of writing) a public water station on your left, where you can fill up your water bottle free of charge.

You should now find yourself back in the main concourse, the gatelines to your far right, and various retailers to your left. Copious seating can also be found as you move down here. Keep a slight look to your left as you move down here, and eventually you will see two plaques on the wall, just before the entrance to the accessible toilet facilities. One triangular shaped one which is a civic trust award, and the other a blue plaque from the Association of railway preservation societies for the 1992 revival of the station.

Turning back, you will see a set of escalators which will take you down to more toilet facilities. Move to the left of these and carry on down. More retail is to your left, with the gatelines across the way to your right. Seating is very prevalent as well. This is nice to see in a station, and hopefully many who do chose to sit, look up and appreciate the architecture around them. Just before you go under the departure board, there is an information desk on your right. Past that on your left are some lifts and another rehydration point, but also on your left here is another statue.

This is also in commemoration of the Kindertransport. It is called 'Fur Das Kind – Displaced', produced by the sculptor Flor Kent and again supported by both the Association of Jewish Refugees (AJR) and World Jewish Relief. It is in tribute to all those who helped with the transportation of 10000 children between 1938/9. It was first dedicated in 2003, and sat in Hope Square when It only had the standing girl. She did however have a large glass case behind her containing artefacts from some of the children who were transported. It was removed from Hope Place in 2006 to enable the current Kindertransport statue to go there. The sitting boy was added the to the girl when, in 2011, it was re-sited to its current location, and at this time it was also re-dedicated. There are two bronze plaques on this statue, one at the front and one at the side, which could do with replacing at they are badly scratched.

As you carry on forward, it is worth looking up at the magnificent roof again, especially if it is a sunny day, just to appreciate how much natural light it gives the interior. The restoration of the pillars is exceptional, the vibrant colours lifting the buildings' aesthetics and really showing what can be done with time and care. The main underground station entrance is to your left, before we get to a set of stairs which will take you up either to the mezzanine or out into Hope Square.

Moving further forward, past cash machines under the stairs, is another exit. This leads into a low ceiling shopping area, much like the other end of the station in feel. Eventually it exits to the bus station. If we now turn back and go back through to the main concourse, you will see that this entrance has that low ceiling. However it really gives the main reveal of the high station roof over the main concourse a real wow factor.

Heading back onto this main area, we shall now review the underground station, which should be a bit forward and to your right.

The underground Station

Being that the terminus is very busy, it is surprising that the underground is quite a modest affair. The entrance from the main concourse is down a set of stairs, however a lift is provided to the left (if you look up you will see the huge war plaque above on the mezzanine). To the far right at the top of the stairs is a visitor centre.

Descending the stairs you will find yourself in a moderately sized area, which is quite pleasant. The ceilings are low, but not intrusive. Information boards are above you are showing arrival and departures. Ticket machines and ATMs can be found to your left here, and the main gatelines are ahead of you. A small coffee shop is far right. The gatelines will either take you to the Hammersmith and City / Circle lines (go straight on), or the Central line (turn to your right).

One thing of note is this is not the only entrance/exit. You can also enter the Underground station via an entrance in Old Broad street. If you were to enter from here, you can go through a set of gatelines, and then down a set of stairs. From there you can turn right for access to platform 2 of the Hammersmith and City / Circle lines (platform 2). Alternatively go left to access platform 1 for the Hammersmith and City /Circle lines. To get to the main station, turn left and continue down the stairs, where you will find the main gateline and access to the National Rail station.

In conclusion

London Liverpool Street station is a fantastic place to visit. The history on show is amazing, and also very thought provoking. I would encourage anyone to come and spend some time here, especially to take a look at the Kindertransport statues, and the majesty of the huge wall plaque dedicated to the railway workers who lost their life during World War One. Many a good photo opportunity can be had overlooking the concourse on the mezzanine level. With the Elizabeth line operating here soon, and new rolling stock on the mainline, the station should have a very bright future.

London Victoria

Opened : *1860*
Platforms : *19*
Underground Lines : *Circle, District, Victoria*
Current TOC's : *Southeastern, Southern, Belmond*
Entry and exit figures 2018/2019 : *74,715,808*

The second busiest station in London (by passenger volume), London Victoria is a well-known terminus for the West End of the city. A bustling, noisy place, which never seems to have a quiet time during the day. This is in part due to the number of services it provides. The ever popular Victoria coach station is adjacent, which carries passengers to and from the station all over the United Kingdom.

The station is also home to the Gatwick Express, currently at time of writing in its 35th year, and this provides passengers from abroad quick access to London. The many other destinations that can be reached give a clue to the origins of the station, which for a time was not one but two termini. These would eventually be brought together when the "big 4" railway companies emerged in the 1920's. It has just undergone a major renovation, mainly to the Underground station, which makes it easier to navigate, and has finally brought the station into the 21st Century.

A brief history

The site which London Victoria sits on was much coveted by the early railway companies. A prime area, close to the West End and the City businesses. Termini already on the south side of the river Thames were not easily accessible to people on the north side of the river, so a terminus on this side would be lucrative.

Eventually, four companies would jointly set up an extension from Battersea on the South side of the river, to a site in the Grosvenor basin. The four companies were The Great Western Railway, London and North Eastern Railway, London Chatham and Dover Railway and London Brighton and South Coast Railway.

The station was called Victoria due to it being on Victoria Street, and was designed by John Fowler, who would later go on to design the Forth railway bridge in Scotland.

The four companies would not stay together long, with the London, Chatham and Dover railway building its own terminus adjacent next to Wilton Road. It was commonly known as the 'Chatham' side, and served the county of Kent. It opened two years after the other side of the station, known as the 'Brighton' side.

The Chatham side had however a very ornate twin span train shed, also designed by John Fowler, The 'Brighton' side would also have a trainshed roof, but this was an unplanned expense due to residence complaints over noise. This had the unfortunate consequence of the façade of the building having to be a rather flat looking wooden structure, instead of the ornate one which was originally planned.

The station would require a new bridge over the river Thames, and this was called the 'Grosvenor Bridge'. It was the first railway bridge to be opened in London. The bridge initially carried only two lines into the station, and John Fowler would again be chosen to be the architect. It was widened in 1866 to four lines, and was constantly increased over the next 100 years, the last being in 1967 when a total of 10 lines were passing over it. Since the mid-20th Century, the south side of the bridge has been dominated by the impressive four towers of Battersea Power Station, now almost fully regenerated into a huge area of homes and leisure facilities.

The two sides of the station would constantly be arguing about whose side was the best. The Chatham side would proclaim that it had the connection to Europe, saying it was "The gateway to the Continent". However it was also seen as the gateway to South East London which was a more working class area than that served by the Brighton side.

The Brighton side would proclaim that it had the 'Southern (later Brighton) Belle' service. This train had far superior carriages than the Chatham side, providing a better level of comfort for the traveller.

A hotel was built and opened in 1862. Called the 'Grosvenor Hotel' it arose on Buckingham Palace Road and was designed by John Knowles, who was a renowned architect known for his elaborate country houses. Its lavish European styled façade impressed and was indeed aimed at the wealthy. However, unlike many other hotels by the railway, it was not owned by any of the four companies. An entrance to and from the Hotel was however built to accommodate customers of the hotel and railway.

A major expansion came to the station in 1902. Taking six years to complete and costing two million pounds, it expanded the Brighton side by eight acres along Buckingham Palace Road. The roof here was also replaced and at last a proper façade was built in an Edwardian style. This did not go unnoticed by the Chatham side however, who in turn updated their front, making it jut out further than the Brighton one with a bigger arched entrance.

The feud between the two was finally ended when, in 1923, the "big four" railway companies were formed. The Southern Railway amalgamated all the companies at Victoria, the dividing wall was removed, and the station become one at last.

Third rail electrification came as early as 1926, with services towards Orpington. More services were added in the next ten years going to West Croydon, Eastbourne and Brighton. The last electrification of the line before the Second World War came in 1939, carrying passengers to the Kent towns of Gillingham and Maidstone on electric trains.

After the war, continuing the theme established in the late 1800's for international travel, a check in desk for a British airline was constructed in 1962. This enabled passengers to check in their luggage before boarding a train to Gatwick where they would fly to Le Touquet in France, then taken via the French train network to Paris, It continued until 1970, when it was withdrawn. However trains still went to Gatwick Airport, and in 1984 the Gatwick Express service started. This still runs today, and is the only train on the UK network to have multi-lingual announcements on board.

During the 2010's, Victoria underwent a major refurbishment to the Underground station, with more step free access points and cleaner, easier to navigate passageways. The forecourt outside the station was also given a makeover, and is now a nice pedestrian area. This also gives good views of both fronts of the station (Chatham and Brighton sides), both of which retain the look of the early 1900's.

The railway station in 2020

Victoria station has a vast array of entrances and exits, but beginning this walkthrough at the 'Chatham' side entrance on the new outdoor pedestrian area seems a good starting point. The Apollo Victoria theatre is to your left as well as a mainly glass walled entrance to the Underground station. Facing toward the railway station entrance you will see on top of the building the sign saying 'Southern Railway' in bronze. Below this to the left and right very ornate sculptures adorn some archways, leading down to the main central arch into the station. This also has a carving above it with two anchors and a crown.

Entering through this archway, the wide spanning trainshed roof is ahead of you, beyond the first main concourse. Also ahead and on the left is the Chatham side departure board, which also contains an advertising screen. Various retail outlets are under this board also. Upon entering the concourse, take a turn to the left and walk down towards the departure board. Note the floor here has different coloured lines, which aim to 'point' you in the right direction. Whether these were added because of the 'mobile generation' is hard to confirm, but it does indicate that most people have their heads down in a station these days!

Food and retail outlets are seen on the right in the station walls as you make your way down between lovely columns which support the roof. Keep moving forward towards a major fast food chain and turn slightly right so that you are going down parallel to the platforms on your right. This is the way down to a gatelines for platforms 1 and 2 . Toilets are to be found halfway down on the left, as well as a couple of ticket machines. The area is quite well looked after, the cream plasterwork works well with the bare brick, and good views of the superb roof can be seen here.

Around three quarters of the way down here is the reception for the Belmond British Pullman, which has a nice pair of clocks above it. This luxury service takes passengers down the Kent coast in heritage carriages, and is normally diesel hauled. Other railtours may also leave from these platforms. Carrying on past down to the gatelines, an exit on your left will take you to the main Station reception, and out onto Bridge Place.

However we shall not take this exit, but instead turn back around and go back towards the 'Chatham' side concourse. Walk forward so that the departure board is on your left, and you will see the main entrance to your right and beyond that on your right an entrance to the Underground station.

Directly ahead is a currency exchange with cash machine, as well as two archways to the left of it. Do not go through these yet, instead take a left turn and move down a wide passageway parallel to platform 7. You will soon have a glass domed retail outlet to your right. These cleverly make use of the other archways and are built through them with the same shape.

This opens out into a wide, pretty and quiet area. The roof stretches out above you and nice wooden seating is provided to your left, with coffee shops to your right. Directly ahead is the left luggage area. When you get to the left luggage area, you will see another platform just on your right.

This is platform 8, which is mostly used during rush hour periods Take the time to look down it past the gateline, the archways extend down it along way, and seem to be still covered in soot in places!

However something of important interest is here at Platform 8. If you look on the right hand wall, you will see a plaque with a wooden frame. This is dedicated to the body of the British unknown warrior, who arrived on the platform on the 10th November 1920, before its interment at Westminster Abbey the next day. The plaque was erected by the Western Front Association, who hold a ceremony at the spot every year on the 10th November.

THE BODY OF THE BRITISH
UNKNOWN WARRIOR
ARRIVED AT PLATFORM 8
AT 8.32pm ON THE
10th NOVEMBER 1920
AND LAY HERE OVERNIGHT
BEFORE INTERMENT
AT WESTMINSTER ABBEY
ON 11th NOVEMBER 1920

Western Front Association

Carry on now through the archway, and you will enter the 'Brighton' side of the station. After a small retail outlet, gatelines for platforms 8 to 12 will appear on your left. Above this is another huge departure board which covers the Brighton side departure and arrivals. Look up to see the difference in the roof, which is more of a greenhouse triangular design. The pillars have good design near the top, with a grey and cream base. Some of these pillars have seating around them.

Continue moving forwards in parallel with the gatelines, and you will soon see the entrance to the Gatwick Express service. Going past this, you will see escalators to your left which take you up to the Victoria Place retail outlet. This is a vast area with shopping and many food outlets, which unlike the outlets on the main concourse, do offer seating. Do not go up these, instead carry on forward, and in front of you above what is currently a currency exchange is a sign carved into the stonework which reads 'Parcel Office'.

Turn to your left here and go down this passageway, noticing a mural on your left which is easily missed as it is inset into a small cut-out area. An exit to the Victoria coach station and Buckingham Palace Road can be found on your right. Continue onto a mini concourse for platforms 15 to 19.

Many retail outlets again can be found here, and three quarters of a way down can be seen departure boards above your head. Passengers are requested to wait here until the platform number for their train is known, and then they can advance to the gateline. This enables arriving passengers to vacate the area first in order to reduce the congestion at this point.

Turn back around and head back to the 'Brighton' side concourse. This is by far the most open concourse in the station, with some seating dotted around so you can appreciate it if you wish. Halfway down here on your left are a brand new set of toilets. Ahead, at the time of writing, is a ticketing office, but if you look above this you will see what used to be a grand entrance to the 'Brighton' side, complete with ornate carvings above the archways.

Walking towards this ticket office, move to your left and above the 'Southern Railway' reception office, you will see a bronze plaque inscribed with 'Refreshment and Dining rooms'. Also note the nicely decorated window above the exit as well. It is always nice to see that these have not been removed.

Do not exit here, instead move back into the main concourse, turning left past the ticket office and then left again once you have passed it. You should now

 be facing a small arched exit. Beside this on the right is a plaque dedicated to those staff members who lost their lives during the First World War, as well as a bronze plaque beneath it dedicated to the staff members who died during the Second World War.

Now go through the archway to the immediate left of the memorial, and if you turn to your right as you go through you will see two tiled maps on the walls at either end. One is a 'Map of System' for the London, Brighton and South Coast Railway, the other a 'Map of suburban lines', also for the London, Brighton and South Coast Railway. It really is brilliant to see that these have been preserved, and are mainly in particularly good condition.

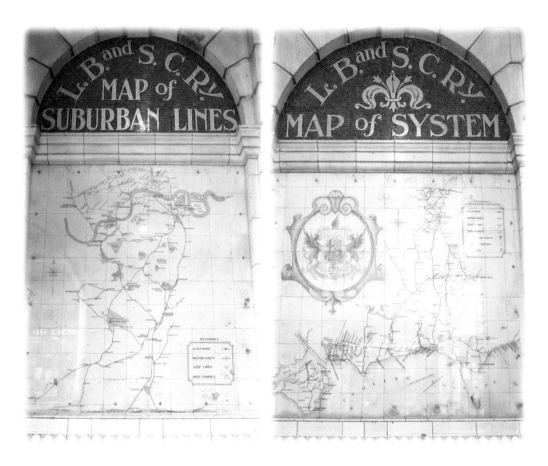

Both maps are beautifully detailed, and it is interesting to see which lines still exist. Obviously, the main lines are there but others, such as the line from Eridge to East Grinstead no longer exist, being subject to the wild cutting of lines after the 1960's Beeching report. Well worth a photo, and if you can, a few more minutes of your time as these maps are such a wealth of information.

Turn back onto the main concourse, and then turn left. You should be heading back towards the mid archways, with the retail area to your right as you do so. You will head back through the arches and back into the 'South Eastern Railway' side of the station. Keep walking towards the arched exit, and beside an information booth next to the archway, you should see a bronze plaque on the pillar. This commemorates the 150th anniversary of the state of Victoria, placed by the Honourable John Cain as a token to the people of Victoria station. This should be where we started, and so concludes the tour of the 2020 station.

The underground station

Victoria station has a few entrances to the Underground station, many of which were added when the underground station was fully refurbished in the late 2010's. This has made the station an incredibly open area, no longer is it a dark and unwelcoming place to use. New exits/entrances give more options, especially the exit at Cardinal place which makes crossing the busy Victoria Street and Wilton road obsolete if you want to get to Westminster City hall or the Cathedral.

Before I explain how to get to the new Cardinal Place entrance, I will take you into the Underground station via the entrance in the main station. If you took the main tour in the previous section, you would have just gone through the arches into the 'SouthEastern railway' side to the station. Looking to your left, you will see the entrance to the Underground, take this and go down the stairs into the Underground station booking hall.

This area is now very airy, a big improvement on the old station which was quite dark and intimidating. Ticketing machines are to your left, with gatelines in front of you, taking you to either the Victoria, Circle or District lines. To your right is a set of stairs taking you up to Wilton Road. Just to the left of the gatelines is a corridor, which will take you to another mini concourse with quicker access to the Circle and District lines. Also exits to Victoria street and up to Terminus place can be found here.

However, let us now look at the new entrance at Cardinal Place. A good warren of tunnels await us, so be prepared to walk a little. This new entrance can be reached as follows. First, if you are not already there, get to the 'Chatham' side entrance, where the main station walkthrough started. Looking ahead, just a little to your right, you will see a large glass building which comes down to the street at a point. For easier recognition, it is the building to the right of the Palace Theatre. Head towards this (you will have to cross a few roads).

After a two to three minute walk, you should see the glass fronted box entrance to the Underground station in Cardinal Place.

The area outside has a few coffee and food outlets, as well as some retail. If you enter this entrance to the Underground, via the steps or the lift, you will be greeted by gatelines, followed by escalators on your right which take you further down. To the left of these, is a small walkway which will take you to a lift which takes you down to the next level also.

If you have taken the escalators, you will see that the modern feeling is accentuated by metal tubing crossing the ceiling at this point. It is very reminiscent of Westminster Underground station, which as a side note is very well worth visiting if you like modern architecture. If you took the lift, take the time to look at the area you come out of and you will see this modern architecture above you.

As you exit the escalators or lift, you should turn left and after a few steps will see an entrance to the Victoria line on your left (a lift down to the platforms is on your right). If you carry on forwards, the walkway turns left again. After a short while the walkway branches off into two. If you take the branch on the right it will take you down a passageway, where at the end you can either turn right and go upstairs to the District and Circle lines, or turn left towards escalators to the Victoria line. Note that there is a lift taking you up to the district and circle line, behind the Victoria line escalators.

However, if you had not taken that branch but carried on you would have seen an exit on your right a little further down. This takes you to exactly the same area, but you will come to the Victoria line escalators first. If however you do not take either branches and carry straight on, a turn to your right will eventually take you to another set of escalators, which will take you to the south ticket hall and the exit to the railway station.

The addition of this entrance / exit is was a much needed access point not only for the underground lines, but to the mainline station. It enables workers or tourists on the far side of the road system to reach Victoria station without the need for crossing the many roads in the area. The step free access to all Underground lines is very welcome also.

In conclusion

London Victoria is a bustling station, which serves a pretty vast area of South and South East England. Many may not realise it was once two separate stations, and just the hint of that era remains due to the differences you can see on the exterior of the buildings.

But old charm still remains, with tiled railway maps and other nods to the past still held on the walls in the concourse. The station has had investment in the Underground station, making getting here from other parts of the country more pleasant. New investment is however long overdue in the railway station itself, but this may come soon in the form of new arrival / departure boards, if the trials go well in late 2020.

Having said that, London Victoria should still be busy regardless of any investment, and the many thousands of people who use it each year will ensure the vibrancy of this station will not be lost in the future.

London Waterloo

Opened : *1848*
Platforms : *24*
Underground Lines : *Bakerloo, Northern, Jubilee, Waterloo & City*
Current TOC : *South Western Railway*
Entry and exit figures 2018/2019 : *94,192,690*

Waterloo station is, at the time of writing (and possibly when you are reading) the busiest footfall station in the United Kingdom, let alone London. It has an impressive original structure which is complimented with a modern area which was once the original London terminus for the Eurostar.

However, there is so much more to see here. From a fantastic main entrance which commemorates the fallen from the two World Wars, to a modern mezzanine which enables you to people watch in comfort. It also boasts probably the most famous station clock in the world, which has featured in many feature films and television shows.

A brief history

The London and Southampton railway had opened section of railway by 1840, and had always aimed to connect the South Coast ports with London. This was to profit from not only from sea traffic, but that of the Thames as well. Its first terminus at Nine Elms, near Battersea, opened in 1838. The company also changed its name at this time to the London and South Western Railway.

The station was, however, a little inconvenient, as passengers needing to access central London would either need to go by boat or by horse and carriage. It also was prone to flooding, and so a new terminus was proposed in 1845 to a site in York road near Waterloo Bridge. A supplementary application was approved in 1847 to allow for more land to be included in the project.

The new station would involve the demolishing of around 700 homes, but would spare the Archbishop of Canterbury's palace at Lambeth by swerving around it. Most of the approach would be on a brick arch and cast iron bridges. It opened for traffic in July 1848 with 3 platforms served by a handful of temporary buildings. The company had intended to move across the river to get to central London. However this idea, on overground lines at least, was never realised.

Two new platforms were built in 1878 to the south of the station. As the Cyprus convention happened in June of that year, as well as the fact that the British Empire was seen as a source of pride for the United Kingdom citizens, this south end soon became known as "Cyprus Station". Co-incidentally, when six new platforms were built on the North side in 1885, General Gordon died in Khartoum. This side of the station would therefore become known as "Khartoum Station". Some people still refer to both these sides as such today, so if someone asks you which way to Cyprus or Khartoum station, just point them in the direction of Waterloo!

The need for the railway to transport passengers north of the river Thames and into the City had not gone away, however. Many schemes were discussed, including an over river crossing, but this was deemed to be too costly. Therefore when a proposal was made to connect Waterloo with the City via an Underground link, investors grew interested. Terms were drawn up which would give investors favourable dividends, and the line got approval from the Government in 1893.

The Waterloo and City line opened in 1898, and proved extremely popular indeed. Due to it only having two stops, and the twisty nature of the line, it quickly got the nickname of "The Drain", something which it keeps to this day. Trains are hoisted in and out of the line via a shaft next to Waterloo. Eventually the London South Western Railway would take complete charge of the line in 1907, and this would remain so until 1994 when London Underground took over ownership of the line.

Moving back to the start of the 20th Century, and Waterloo Station was beginning to get terribly busy. This was because not only did it cater for the blossoming commuter market, but also served long distance journeys to the south coast. Unfortunately, the station was quite hard to navigate, with bridges and alleyways a plenty, and a platform numbering system that for some reason did not run sequentially.

For this reason, a plan by the LWSR board to re-organize the station was put forward. This would involve a complete demolition of the current station buildings, and slums to the south of the station. This took some time, but eventually five new platforms would be opened in 1909. The main refurbishment of the buildings and roof were started by architect J.W Jacomb-Hood (and completed by A.W Szlumper after Jacomb-Hoods death in 1914). After many delays due to the First World War, the whole project was eventually completed in 1922.

It was, however, worth it. Passengers entering the station from what is known now as Cab Street, were greeted with a grand new entrance known as "Victory Arch", by the architect J.R. Scott. It is a fitting commemoration to the railway workers who were killed during World War One, and remains one of the most spectacular entrances to any terminus. The rest of the station sweeps in a crescent, and surprisingly these buildings were not a railway hotel, but instead offices for the railway. Inside, the concourse was huge at 800 ft long. The platforms were also better organised, at last in sequential order.

The installation of the famous four face clock was also completed at this time. Many have used it as a meeting point, and it has a reputation for being the place to meet a loved one (new or otherwise) due to its prominent position high in the centre of the concourse. A full refurbishment of it by Gents' of Leicester was finished in 2010, ensuring the clock works well into the future.

Another feature of the station came in 1930, with the installation of a mini cinema at Platform 1. This showed news-reels and cartoons, and was quite popular. No doubt the popularity of a similar cinema in London Victoria Station which opened a year before influence the decision to open one here. Unfortunately, it showed its last film in 1970 and was demolished in 1988.

A major extension to the station occurred in the 1990's when it was decided that Waterloo would be the terminus of the new Eurostar train service to and from Europe. This was only meant to be a stop-gap however, whilst the wrangling and eventual construction of High Speed 1 was taking place. Once that was built, Eurostar services transferred to St Pancras International in November of 2007.

It would be almost 12 years until the old Eurostar re-opened, this time as extra capacity for the station. Mainly carrying suburban routes, this expansion was needed as Waterloo's footfall kept increasing. The old Eurostar terminal underneath the platforms is being changed into retail space, and also an extra entrance and exit to the Underground.

The railway station in 2020

This tour will start at the elaborate entrance (known as 'The Victory Arch) in Cab Road. But before we start, take a moment to go across the road via the zebra crossing and enter the arch in front of you. In here you will see some mosaics, which invite you either to go to the bus station or one which just says 'to the trains'. Also here is an introduction to 'William Blake' who lived in the area between 1890 and 1900. The mosaics here are part of a collection, and the information here gives an idea where you can go to see the rest of them (70 in total within a Kilometre of here). In my opinion, this arched mini tunnel houses some real hidden gems and they could easily be overlooked if you were rushing from the bus on Waterloo road to get to the station.

Let us now go back across the crossing and walk towards the impressive entrance to Waterloo station. Sited on Cab Road, this entrance is well worth five minutes of your time. Constructed to commemorate the First World War, it is known as the 'Victory Arch' and was designed by James Rob Scott. It is first topped by statue of Britannia. Below this the words 'Waterloo Station' stand out in black type against the grey stonework.

Moving your eyes further down, you will now see an arch decorated with carved stone pieces (more on these later). These then take the eye past a glass arch and then to a spectacular clock. Either side of the entrance, two huge and thick columns stand proud. The one on the left inscribed '1914' and has a figure depicting Bellona (the Roman goddess of war) with sword and torch on top. A rectangular window with a pillared double lantern in front is below the inscription.

The column to the right has '1918' inscribed and has a figure of Pax (the goddess of peace) sitting on Earth. It too has a rectangular window and pillared double lantern. This is surely one of the most elaborate entrances to any of the London termini, and is a shame it is not seen by many, especially if they arrive by the London Underground.

Getting closer to the archway, you will be able to read on the arch above the clock the words *'Dedicated to the employees of the company who fell in the war'.* Immediately above this are reliefs which contain the names Belgium, Italy, Dardanelles, France, Mesopotamia, Egypt and North Sea. In-between the names various carvings to do with the war are shown, such as rifles, helmets and cannon. Although today protected by a wire mesh, the detail can still be seen, and looks as if it has been kept in pristine condition.

Moving to the columns, as said each contains a pillar which as a silver plaque adoring it. Both are engraved with the S&WR logo set within a circle. A black relief goes either side, and is styled very subtly in the form of a railway track. These lead to two impressive lanterns either side, also finished in black and silver metal. Small lion heads are attached near the top of this pillar and it is finished by a metal star shaped lantern on the top.

Moving up the stairs, to your left is a roll of honour plaque dedicated to the employees who lost their lives in the first world war. It is mirrored with further names on your right. As you get to the top of the stairs, turn right and go across the landing to the other side. Two plaques are located here. One a bronze in commemoration of the 50th anniversary of D-Day, which was dedicated by Railtrack South West. The other nearest the door is a small dedication to the men of the Southern Railway who lost their lives in the Second World War.

As you move through the glass doors, which at time of writing have the network Rail logo on them, you will see two further Rolls of Honour either side, again dedicated to the employees who lost their lives in the First World War.

As you go through into the main concourse, turn around and look up at the archway. It has an exit sign in gold, with semi-circular glazing just above.

Keep facing this way and move towards a plaque on your left. This is dedicated to Herbert Ashcombe Walker, who was the London and South Western Railway General Manager, and well as the Southern Railway general manager. It celebrates his achievements in the re-development of Southampton docks and the electrification of the Southern Railway.

I must say that this particular plaque could be overlooked, as the writing really needs repairing, the bottom especially is getting quite faded. I do hope this can be restored, as it would be a shame to lose such a dedication to a man who obviously was key to the success of the railway in the south of England.

Turning to your left, you will see an exit which will take you to the South Bank area near the River Thames. Keep turning around and you will see the impressive glass structure which was originally constructed to house the Eurostar terminal. As said in the history, this operated between 1994 and 2007, when St Pancras International took over the service. However it was fully re-opened in May 2019 to help cope with the increased traffic in and out of Waterloo. The excellent walkway up to the gateline really is fully accessible, and the flooding in of natural light makes this area very pleasant indeed.

Start to move up this ramp, and if you look to your left and over the barrier, you will see a further concourse area which leads to the old terminal area for Eurostar, more on this a little later.

Moving on up the ramp onto the concourse area, you will notice how it is noticeably big and open. Ahead of you there is a large departure board above the platform gatelines. These allow access to platforms 20 through to 24, which have services to places such as Reading, Windsor and Eton and a 'circular' service which takes in places such as Twickenham, Chiswick and Putney. This has allowed an increase in suburban services, which in turn should help the expected footfall increases at Waterloo.

It is worth having a good look at the impressive roof when you are up here, it lets in so much natural light and is quite high. Accented with blue on the metal which stops it from becoming just another glass roof in my opinion. Some may see it as out of place compared with the original roof over the rest of the station, but personally I think it is elegant.

Once you have finished up on this concourse, turn back around and start to go down the ramp, noticing the lifts to your left just before you descend. Once you reach the main concourse, head towards the gents toilet in front of you, to the right of a retail outlet. As you do so, you will see a green plaque on a pillar to the left of the last entrance of that retail outlet.

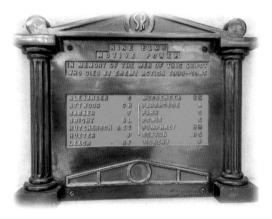

The plaque is small and can be easily missed. It is dedicated to the men of the Nine Elms Motive Power depot, who lost their lives in the Second World War. An unusual looking plaque and well worth a look.

Turning around now 180 degrees, so that you have the sloped entrance to the new platforms to your right, and an Underground entrance to your left. If you head towards the Underground entrance, you will soon see steps on your right which take you down to the lower concourse we saw earlier on the ramp. Take these steps down to this lower area.

After exiting the steps, turn towards the left. You will see steps ahead of you which will take you up to the new platforms. To the left of this is an entrance to some very nice toilet facilities, which seem to be a throwback to the Eurostar days as they are very opulent for a railway station! As you look to the right of the stairs, you will see a corridor (more on that in a moment) and to the right of that a set of lifts will take you either to the new platforms or down to the Underground station for Waterloo and City, Bakerloo and Northern lines. Further to the right is another exit to the South Bank.

If you wish to, move forward and enter into the walkway which goes under the new platforms. At time of writing this had nothing adorning it but white walls, but the plan is for this to be an extensive retail space. At the end of the corridor in an open space, are escalators taking you down to the Underground station. Once you have had a look around here, go back out, and head up the steps you descended earlier to the main concourse once more.

Once here, you will notice a set of gatelines in front of you. Now turn to your left and head back to the green plaque we saw earlier. Once there, turn to your right and continue walking. You will walk past the gents toilets on your left, followed by a coffee retailer and then female and disability toilets, also on your left.

Next to these are a set of escalators which take you to the buses and a way out to Tenison Way. You will see a side of an escalator to your right, with seating around it. Once you see the bottom of these escalators, move slightly to your right, so that you start to move down the middle of the concourse. More retail can be seen on your left as you walk down, as well as the gatelines for the platforms on your right. There are automatic ticket machines in the centre of the concourse, as we make out way towards the clock above.

Once you are standing under the clock, you will soon realise why this is such an iconic part of the station. The four clock faces look out across the station, as if drawing you towards them. No wonder people have for years used this as a meeting place, you can see it from virtually every point of the main concourse. We shall get a closer look at the clock when we ascend to the mezzanine level shortly.

Under the clock is an information desk, as well as a newspaper retailer. As you start again to move forward, more automatic ticket machines are in the middle, and further retail can be seen to the left under the mezzanine level. Shortly you will see a currency exchange ahead of you, walk past this and then turn around to see an entrance to the Underground here, right in the middle of the concourse, opposite gatelines for Platforms 7 and 8. This will take you down to the Jubilee, Northern, Waterloo and City, and Bakerloo lines.

Carry on forward now towards the back end of the station, and when you see the gatelines for Platforms 1 to 5 on your right, an entrance to the Underground for the Jubilee line is to your left. If you were to carry on walking straight ahead here, you will eventually reach an exit for Westminster Bridge road. However, you should see a set of escalators in front of you, just after the entrance to the Underground station. Take these up to the mezzanine level. When at the top, turn to your left and start walking down this elevated walkway.

Cafes and eateries are to your right as you walk down, as well as seating to your left. After a little while you will soon see on your left a round plaque on the wall surrounded by marble. This is a memorial to the Allied Armies who died at the Battle of Waterloo. It also has a quote from First Field Marshall, Arthur Wellesley, beneath.

Turning back to walk down the walkway, you will soon pass another escalator on your left, with some glass panels further to your left which give good views of the bustling concourse below. If you have chosen to take a look over the concourse here, once you have finished, move back to the walkway and continue moving forward. Almost immediately you will notice some lifts on your right, followed by an exit to Waterloo East Station.

Carry on forward and you will go past a café on your left, which will soon give you an eye level view of the clock. However, face way from the clock and on the wall behind you is a very interesting piece of the station. Here you will see a stone arch, with a stained glass window inset. To the left and right of it are names of counties that are, or were, served by the station. The insignia of the London and South Western Railway sits above these names.

Above the top of the arch is a cherub type figurehead, and if you look at the stained glass below it, you will see the coat of arms of the London and South Western Railway. Moving towards the glass barrier here, look down beneath the window, and you will find that this is an arch for the exit to the road called 'Station Approach' below you. Because of the mezzanine, you cannot now see this from the main concourse. Take a little time to appreciate this original part of the building, as it is well preserved.

Once you have finished, turn to your left and continue down the walkway a little until you can stand by the glass panels to your left. Not only can you get a good look at the station from here, but it offers a great place to view the clock (if you cannot get a seat in the café that is!).

Continue on down the mezzanine when you are ready, past more retail on your left and eventually you will reach the end, where an escalator will take you back down to the main concourse. If you look to your left once you have reached the bottom, you will see an entrance to the Underground station for the Waterloo and City, Bakerloo and Northern lines.

Normally this would be the end of the tour, but Waterloo has a hidden treasure which can only be reached during certain hours. There is an underground walkway which links all the platforms. It can be reached by sets of steps on the platforms, a little walk away from the main gatelines, or by the Underground stations. It is here to relieve congestion during the peak times.

But also down in this underground walkway is a 'hidden' plaque. It is to be found between platforms 11 and 13, and commemorates the 'Waterloo free buffet' which was provided for soldiers and sailors of the First World War. It was entirely run by volunteers and fed over eight million men. If you have a ticket to travel, try to get down and see this hidden gem, which many people would rush past in order to get their train.

The underground station

Waterloo has a few entrances to the Underground station. Most are quite standard with automated ticketing machines on the wall, and gatelines through to the platforms. However, you need to be mindful that the entrances by the high platform numbers will only take you to the Northern, Waterloo and City, and Bakerloo lines. To reach the Jubilee line you need to make your way to the lower platform numbers.

The one entrance however which is worth a look is the one opposite platforms 1-5, which is for the Jubilee line only. Descend the escalator, and turn to your left. After a little walk, you will enter quite a big concourse, with gatelines ahead of you. But your eyes will be drawn to the sculpture between the escalators down to the platforms.

Yes, it is a sculpture of an elephant, coming out of the wall. The sculpture was created by Kendra Haste, for the 'Platform for Art' Programme. When that programme finished, London Underground bought the elephant and put it here. The question is, why? Well a popular theory is that the site of the world's first circus ring was on a site now occupied by St Thomas' hospital nearby. Another theory put forward is that it faces towards the Elephant and Castle area of London. Whatever the reason, it is certainly worth a look, just for the novelty value alone.

In conclusion

London Waterloo never seems to be quiet. Passengers arrive and depart at all hours, whether it be for work or pleasure. The huge number of platforms confirms its place as one of the busiest stations in the world. Yet, it still can surprise, with either hidden plaques, or not so hidden elephants.

A mix of old and new, the station is developing into a place to visit, not just to travel to and from. History can be found if you take the time to look around you, because not everything is in plain sight. The refurbished world famous clock is a statement that this terminus is ready as a meeting place for everyone, no matter where their journey may take them. And the Impressive 'Victory Arch' stands proud as a reminder of sacrifices past, that let us enjoy our future.

Covid -19

Nobody could have predicted what would happen to the world during 2020. A pandemic spread across the globe, bringing entire nations to a halt. Transport systems were one of the worst hit areas, with reduced capacity due to social distancing. Couple that with national and local lockdowns and travel by rail reduced dramatically virtually overnight. By the 3rd quarter of the year, rail networks were mostly opened up again, but still with reduced capacity.

Despite all this, the railways kept on running, with measures put in place to make the journeys as safe as possible not only for passengers, but also the staff. It produced a totally different landscape, especially in London. In July 2020, I visited London for a 'clear up' trip for this book, and was amazed how quiet the termini and Underground were. Signs for social distancing and hand sanitising were everywhere, as well as safety notices. But some nice touches were to be found too. I have included in this last section some images of that trip, in order to preserve some of the things seen in the London termini at that time.

Carry hand sanitiser and wash your hands before and after travelling

Wear a face covering

Please keep your distance

Please keep your distance

LET'S KEEP SAFE TOGETHER
Let's all do our bit to travel safely during the coronavirus outbreak.
Plan ahead. Consider others. Stay safe.

Go **online** to book tickets and use **contactless** payments wherever possible

Carry **hand sanitiser** and **wash your hands** before and after travelling

LET'S KEEP SAFE TOGETHER

Let's all do our bit to travel safely during the coronavirus outbreak.

WE ARE:

Putting on more trains where possible to help you travel safer.

Doing more antiviral deep cleaning, especially on touched surfaces.

Putting on more staff to help you get around the station safely and easily.

Placing signage and floor markings to help you keep a safe distance.

Providing hand sanitiser in key journey spots to help you stay germ-free.

YOU CAN:

Plan ahead and check live train times to be extra prepared.

Avoid touching surfaces if possible, when it is safe to do so.

Follow staff advice and think of others who may need help.

Wear a face covering to avoid putting others at risk of infection.

Wash your hands more frequently and use hand sanitiser if possible.

Members of the public were invited to send in railway rainbow pictures to brighten up the station during the Covid-19 crisis in 2020

The following pictures were taken between 1500 and 1600, normally such stations would be a hive of activity.

Bibliography

Books

Bownes, David with Oliver Green and Sam Mullins – *Underground : How the Tube Shaped London,* 2012
Christopher, John – *London's Historic Railways Through Time,* 2015
Green, Oliver – *The Tube,* 2012
Heather, Chris – *London Railway Stations,* 2018
Jackson, Alan – *London's Termini,* 1969
Jenkins, Simon – *Britain's 100 Best Railway Stations,* 2017
Marshall, Geoff – *Tube Station Trivia,* 2018
Ovenden, Mark - *London Underground By Design,* 2013

World Wide Web

https://en.wikipedia.org/wiki/Midland_Railway
https://stpancras.com/about-st-pancras/history
https://stpancras.com/about-st-pancras/history/decay-and-restoration
https://www.thameslinkprogramme.co.uk/london-bridge
https://www.londonremembers.com/memorials/ww1-at-liverpool-street-station
https://yoursculpture.wordpress.com/2015/09/14/fur-das-kind-at-liverpool-street-station/
https://www.subbrit.org.uk/sites/moorgate-station/
https://en.wikipedia.org/wiki/Moorgate_station
https://profjoecain.net/euston-grove-history-of-a-london-street-nw1/
https://en.wikipedia.org/wiki/Copenhagen_Tunnel
https://www.ianvisits.co.uk/blog/2020/02/05/new-images-of-london-undergrounds-new-paddington-entrance/
https://journeytojustice.org.uk/wp/wpcontent/uploads/2018/04/AsquithXavier_factsheet.pdf

All photographs shown within this book were taken by myself.

Sculptures, Statues and items of interest

Cannon Street
Sculpture - 'The Plumbers Apprentice' – **Martin Jennings**

Charing Cross
Northern line mural by **David Gentleman** (davidgentleman.com)

Euston
Statue of Robert Louis Stevenson - **Carlo Marochetti**

Kings Cross
Plaque with words from poem "The Whitsun Weddings" by **Philip Larkin**
Statue of Sir Nigel Gresley by **Hazel Reeves**

Liverpool Street
Sculpture – 'Children of the Kindertransport' – **Frank Meisler & Aire Ovadia**
Sculpture – 'Fur Das Kind' – **Flor Kent**
Both of the above sculptures at Liverpool Street are supported by, and
reproduced in this book by kind permission of **The Association of Jewish
Refugees** and **World Jewish Relief**

Paddington
Sculpture of Paddington Bear – **Marcus Cornish**
Paddington Bear bench – **Michelle Heron**
War Memorial Sculpture – **Charles Sargeant Jagger**
Statue of Isambard Kingdom Brunel – **John Doubleday**

St Pancras International
Sculpture – "The Meeting Place" – **Paul Day**
Installation – "I Want My Time With You" – **Tracey Emin**
Statue of Sir John Betjeman by **Martin Jennings**

Waterloo
Jubilee Line sculpture – 'Elephant' - **Kendra Haste**

Index

ABOUT THE AUTHOR

John Jones is a railway enthusiast who is from North Kent, England. He has always had an interest in railways, in particular the infrastructure which makes it all run. He owns, and posts to his own blog, Rainham Rail Enthusiast, which also has its own YouTube channel. John is currently a member of the East Kent Railway, based at Shepherdswell, Kent.

As well as life size railways, John enjoys his static OO gauge railway, 'Mistydale' which he posts updates on to the Mistydale Facebook page.

He is married with two sons, and gained a BSc (Hons) Degree in Technology from the Open University in 2015.

For more information, and to view videos from John Jones, search for 'Rainham Rail Enthusiast' on YouTube, Facebook and Instagram.

www.rainhamrailenthusiast.com
www.youtube.com/rainhamrailenthusiast

Printed in Great Britain
by Amazon